Basic Skills for the TOEFL® iBT

Jeff Zeter

Compass Publishing

Writing 2

Basic Skills for the TOEFL® iBT 2

Writing

Jeff Zeter

© 2008 Compass Publishing

Project Editor: Liana Robinson
Acquisitions Editor: Emily Page
Content Editor: Michael Jones
Copy Editor: Jenna Myers
Contributing Writers: David Charlton, Warren Franklin
Consultants: Lucy Han, Chanhee Park
Cover/Interior Design: Dammora Inc.

email: info@compasspub.com
http://www.compasspub.com

ISBN: 978-1-59966-158-2

10 9 8 7 6 5 4
10

Contents

What is the TOEFL® test?

The TOEFL® iBT (Test of English as a Foreign Language Internet-based Test) is designed to assess English proficiency in non-native speakers who want to achieve academic success as well as effective communication. It is not meant to test academic knowledge or computer ability; therefore, questions are always based on material found in the test.

The TOEFL® iBT test is divided into four sections:
- Reading
- Speaking
- Listening
- Writing

TOEFL® Scores

TOEFL® scores can be used for:
- Admission into university or college where instruction is in English
- Employers or government agencies who need to determine a person's English ability
- English-learning institutes that need to place students in the appropriate level of English instruction

It is estimated that about 4,400 universities and other institutions require a certain TOEFL® test score for admission.

The exact calculation of a TOEFL® test score is complicated and not necessary for the student to understand. However, it is helpful to know that:
- Each section in the Internet-based test is worth 30 points
- The highest possible score on the iBT is 120 points
- Each institution will have its own specific score requirements

✳ It is very important to check with each institution individually to find out what its admission requirements are.

Registering for the TOEFL® iBT

Students who wish to take the TOEFL® test must get registration information. Registration information can be obtained online at the ETS website. The Internet address is www.ets.org/toefl.

The website provides information such as:
- testing locations
- identification requirements
- registration information
- costs
- other test preparation material
- test center locations

This information will vary depending on the country in which you take the test. Be sure to follow the requirements carefully. If you do not have the proper requirements in order, you may not be able to take the test. Remember that if you register online, you will need to have your credit card information ready.

Introduction to the Writing Section of the TOEFL® iBT

The writing section of the test is designed to assess your ability to organize and support your ideas in essay format and use English correctly. You will have two writing tasks. One task is based both on a reading and on a lecture. You will be required to summarize the information you have heard and to relate the information heard in the lecture to the information in the passage. This is called Integrated Writing. The second task requires you to generate an essay based on your own experience. You will be given no material to work with; it will be based completely on your own ideas. This is called Independent Writing.

Question Types

Questions for the writing section of the TOEFL® iBT will appear in the following order:

Question	Type	Time	Response Length	Description
1	Integrated: 250-300 word reading 250-300 word lecture	20 minutes	150-225 words	Compare or contrast information presented in the reading passage with information presented in the lecture
2	Independent	30 minutes	300+ words	Present a personal opinion or describe an experience, including details and examples

How Writing Will Be Scored

ETS graders will score test takers' essays for writing tasks according to the following scale:

Score	General Description	Key Points
5	The **integrated** essay includes important information from both the reading and the lecture and appropriately explains the information with regard to the prompt. The **independent** essay answers the question well and the ideas are fully developed.	The essay is easy to understand and is well organized. There is good use of language, correct choice of words, and idioms to express ideas. Minor errors in grammar and word choice are acceptable.
4	The **integrated** essay includes most of the key points from the reading and the lecture as they relate to the prompt, but not all of the points are fully explained. The **independent** essay can be understood and answers the question, but not all of the ideas are fully developed.	There is good use of language, including an appropriate range of sentence structure and vocabulary. There are several minor errors with language, or some ideas may not seem connected, but these errors do not make comprehension difficult.
3	The **integrated** essay does not include or correctly explain a key point from the lecture or reading, or shows only a limited understanding of the information. The **independent** essay gives a basic answer to the question, but not many examples or details are provided.	Errors in sentence structure, grammar, and word choice may make the meaning of some sentences vague or difficult to comprehend. Transitions or connections between ideas are not always easy to follow. However, the important ideas in the essay can be understood.
2	The **integrated** essay does not include sufficient information from the reading, lecture, or both and the reader cannot follow connections between ideas. The **independent** essay is very short and not well organized. The ideas are not connected and examples are not explained.	Errors in sentence structure, grammar, and word choice appear in almost every sentence and make ideas in the essay difficult to understand in key points; readers unfamiliar with the reading and lecture/prompt may not be able to follow the essay.
1	The **integrated** essay includes few or none of the key points. The essay is poorly written and difficult to understand. The **independent** essay is short and confusing. Little or no detail is given to support ideas, and irrelevant information is included.	Frequent and serious errors in grammar and word choice make sentences in the essay impossible to understand.
0	The essay only copies words from the prompt or is not related to the topic at all.	Not enough of the student's writing is available to score.

Test Management

- Before you begin the writing section, listen to the headset directions. It is very important that you can hear clearly during the lectures.

- Note-taking is permitted. Paper will be provided by the test supervisor. These notes can be studied when preparing your response.

- If you miss something that is said in a lecture, do not panic. Forget about it and simply keep listening. Even native speakers do not hear everything that is said.

- The reading passage disappears while listening and reappears after listening, so don't worry about taking notes on all of the key points in the reading. You will NOT be able to hear the listening again, so it is very important to take good notes while you listen.

- You have to type in your answers. You can use icon buttons at the top of the screen for editing. The editing tools include copy, cut, and paste.

- Keep the style of essay writing in English in mind. First, select a main idea, explain it clearly, then support and develop it using details and/or examples. Be sure your essay has a logical flow. There should be a reason for every sentence in your essay, such reasons include introducing a new example or detail to support the main idea, or explaining or supporting an example or detail mentioned previously. Do not write any sentences that are unrelated to your main idea or that do not fit into the organizational structure of your essay just to increase your word count.

- Make every effort to use effective language and appropriate sentence structure and vocabulary. Try NOT to use vocabulary or constructions that you are not confident with, as these will increase your chances of making errors.

- Use a variety of language. English has a large number of synonyms and analogous constructions, so using the same construction repeatedly is considered poor style.

- Keep the 50-minute time limit for the entire writing section in mind. Remember that raters are expecting to read drafted essays, not finely-polished final products. If you find yourself stuck in a particular part of your essay, it is best to move on and complete the essay, then go back and fix the difficult area.

- Try to leave at least five minutes for revision. When revising, be sure to look for spelling or grammatical errors (remember, there is no spell checker on the test!) as well as ways to improve the structure and flow of your essay.

- You must answer each question as it appears. You can NOT return to any questions later.

- Do not leave any question unanswered. You are NOT penalized for guessing an answer.

[01] Independent

Getting Ready to Write

A. Learn the words.

Key Vocabulary

valuable	having value or importance
spoil	to weaken by treating too well
cheer (someone) up	to make a sad person feel happy
otherwise	differently

TOEFL® Vocabulary

component	a part or piece of something
attempt	to try to do something
sympathy	the condition of knowing the feelings of another
suffer	to feel pain
relieve	to lessen a feeling of pain or sickness

B. Read the prompt. Then answer the questions.

> Describe an animal that makes a good pet.

1. What kind of animal makes the best pet?
   The best animal for a pet is _____.

2. What do you like about that animal?
   I like _____.

3. Why does that animal make a good pet?
   It is a good pet because _____
   _____.

4. How would your family feel about having this animal as a pet?
   My family would _____.

Practice

A. Read the question.

Do you agree or disagree with the following statement?

Pets are just as important as family members.

Use specific reasons and examples to support your answer.

B. Read the sample response. Then answer the question.

I think that pets are very important members of the family. In fact, they are just as valuable as each person in a family. There are two main reasons for this. The first is that a pet is an important component of many families. Many people attempt to include their pets in their daily lives and special events. Pets are included as if they are the same as any other family member. For example, in my family we like our dogs to watch TV with us. We also take them on picnics with us. Second, pets can give sympathy to humans, just like a friend or a family member does. Dogs are very good at knowing when a person is suffering or lonely. If I am feeling sad, my dogs will try to cheer me up. When I play with them, it relieves me of my sadness. Therefore, I think that pets are very important family members.

Which side of the statement does the response take?
(A) Agree   (B) Disagree

C. Complete the outline for the response.

Topic: Pets are _____ members of the family.
A. A pet is _____
   1. Many people attempt to _____
   2. In my family, we like our dogs _____
B. Pets can give _____
   1. Dogs are good at knowing _____
   2. When I am sad, my dogs _____
   3. When I play with them, it _____
Conclusion: I think that _____.

D. Underline the transitional words or phrases in the sample response.

E. Read the sample response. Then answer the question.

I don't understand why so many people treat their pets the same as family members. Pets are not the same as other family members. To think otherwise is a mistake. First of all, pets do not contribute anything to the family. To be in a family is to contribute by doing things like washing dishes or cooking dinner. Only people can do these things. Pets are nice, but their only jobs are to eat, to sleep, and to play. Secondly, some people spoil their pets. I've seen many people treat their pets with lots of sympathy and kindness. But then those same people are unfriendly to their family members. It is sad not to care about improving your relationships with your family. The whole family suffers when you give pets too much importance. For these reasons, I think it is not good to treat pets as importantly as other family members.

Which side of the statement does the response take?

(A) Agree   (B) Disagree

F. Complete the outline for the response.

Topic: Pets are _____ as other family members.
A. Pets do not contribute _____
   1. Family members should contribute by doing things like _____
   2. The only job of pets is to _____
B. Some people spoil their pets but are unfriendly _____
   1. It is sad not to care for your _____
   2. The whole family suffers when you _____
Conclusion: I think it is not good to treat pets _____.

G. Underline the transitional words or phrases in the sample response.

H. Fill in the blanks with the correct words.

attempt	relieve	component	suffer	sympathy

1. The soccer player scored a goal on his first _____.
2. It is important to carefully check each _____ before putting them together.
3. The nurse told him to take two aspirin to _____ the symptoms of his headache.
4. Families that have _____ for each other are often stronger and happier than families that don't.
5. If you do not study for your test, you are likely to _____ serious consequences like failing the class.

Test

Step 1

Read the question.

Do you agree or disagree with the following statement?

Pets are just as important as family members.

Use specific reasons and examples to support your answer.

Step 2

State your opinion.

I _____ with the statement.

Step 3

Write an outline for your essay that will support your opinion.

Topic: Pets are _____ as important as family members.

A. _____

    1. _____

    2. _____

B. _____

    1. _____

    2. _____

Conclusion: _____.

Step 4

Complete the response using your outline from above.

    I think that pets are _____ members of a family.

There are two reasons why _____.

First, I think this because _____

_____.

For example, _____

_____.

Second, pets also _____. For instance, _____

_____

_____

_____.

It is for these reasons that I think _____

_____.

Integrated - History

Getting Ready to Write

A. Learn the words.

Key Vocabulary

fall	the weakening or defeat of something
troops	people in the military; soldiers
loyal	willing to support without quitting
invade	to take an army into a country to attack it

TOEFL® Vocabulary

decline	to become worse
stability	a state in which few things go wrong
sustain	to keep something going
external	coming from outside
infrastructure	the set of systems that lets something work correctly

Reading Passage

B. Read the first part of a passage. Then answer the questions.

The Fall of Rome

The fall of Rome happened slowly—and it happened from within. The main cause was Rome's poor military. Rome's empire began to decline in 200 CE. Its stability declined due to its failure to manage the military. Two major faults stopped Rome from sustaining its hold over its land.

1. What is the main idea of the passage?

   (A) Why the Roman Empire fell
   (B) The effects of Rome's fall

2. What do you think the rest of the passage will talk about? Write two or three ideas below.

   _____

   _____

Practice

A. Listen to the first part of a lecture. Then answer the question. `Track 1`

What is the main idea of the lecture?

(A) Comparing two types of ancient militaries

(B) Two external reasons for the fall of Rome

B. Read the full passage. Then listen to the full lecture. Take notes in the boxes below. `Track 2`

The Fall of Rome

The fall of Rome happened slowly—and it happened from within. The main cause was Rome's poor military. Rome's empire began to decline in 200 CE. Its stability declined due to its failure to manage the military. Two major faults stopped Rome from sustaining its hold over its land.

First, Rome lacked a strong military leader. Earlier, Rome was led by smart soldiers. However, in 196 CE, Rome's leadership changed. Commodus became Rome's ruler. He was a mean and careless leader. Most of the Roman troops did not like him. Thus, Rome lost many battles. Their troops lacked a good leader.

In addition, fewer Romans joined the army. With a bad leader, fewer people wanted to fight. The military leaders began to hire troops from other countries. These troops were not loyal to Rome. Thus, they fought only for money. They did not fight like Rome's soldiers in the past that fought because they loved Rome.

Reading

Main idea: Rome fell because of its military.
Key points:
  - Rome did not have a good _____
  - Not many people wanted to _____

Lecture

Main idea: External military forces caused the fall of Rome.
Key points:
  - The Persians captured _____, which hurt Rome's military.
    - Rome's troops were no longer as _____
    - It also _____ from Rome.
  - Barbarians attacked _____
    - This _____ Rome's infrastructure.
    - It also hurt _____

C. Read the prompt.

Summarize the main points made in the lecture and explain how they differ from the main points in the reading passage.

D. Fill in the blanks of the sample response using phrases from the box. Use your notes to help you.

The reading explains why Rome fell. The author says Rome fell because it had _____. There are two reasons why this is true.

First, Rome did not have _____. One leader, Commodus, was especially bad. Even _____ did not like him. This made the military weak.

Second, the soldiers did not want to fight. Most people only fought because they _____. The army became weak because of this.

The lecture, though, said that other militaries attacked Rome and caused it to fall. The Persians often attacked the Roman Empire. During one attack, they _____. This hurt Rome's confidence. In addition, barbarians attacked the empire.

One group called the Goths often attacked. _____ they stole money and weakened Rome. These attacks caused Rome to fall.

a bad military	good leaders
The author says	captured the Roman leader
wanted money	the Roman troops

E. Fill in the blanks with the correct words.

decline   stability   sustain   external   infrastructure

1. The Internet works because of a huge _____ of connected computers.

2. Many people say that someone's personality is more important than his or her _____ features.

3. There has been a(n) _____ in crime in the area after the police began to guard it.

4. Runners find it hard to _____ a fast pace through a long race.

5. The economy lost its _____ when the stock market crashed.

Test

Step 1

Read the passage. Then listen to the lecture. Take notes in the boxes below. **Track 3**

The Decline of the Roman Economy

Many economic problems caused Rome to fall. At first, Rome had a very stable economy. However, that changed in the third century. Goths began to invade Roman lands. Their attacks had many effects. For one, the Goth troops stole many items. They also destroyed towns and ports. This made it harder to trade in Europe.

The Romans began to trade in Asia. This was much more expensive. Rome spent large amounts of money buying items from Asia. As a result, Rome became less wealthy. In addition, the prices in Rome went up. Roman leaders realized they were losing money. They began to reduce the value of their money. Coins then became worth much less than in the past. Prices then went up sharply.

Over time, Rome could not sustain itself due to high prices. Without money, the empire could not continue.

Reading

Main idea: Rome fell because of problems with the economy.
Key points:
- The Goths began _____
  - Made it harder _____
- Rome became _____
- The prices _____

Lecture

Main idea: Rome's political troubles caused its fall.
Key points:
- Commodus became leader because _____
  - This was a mistake because _____
  - He did not have much _____
- One of Rome's leaders _____
  - This started a _____
  - It allowed the _____

Step 2

Read and listen to the prompt. **Track 4**

Summarize the main points made in the lecture and explain how they differ from the main points in the reading passage.

Step 3

Complete the outline using your notes from Step 1.

Topic: The causes of the fall of Rome.

A. The reading says Rome fell because of _____

   1. The Goths began _____

   2. The prices _____

B. The lecture says Rome's _____ caused its fall.

   1. Commodus became leader because _____

     • He was not _____

     • He did not have much _____

   2. One of Rome's leaders _____

     • Started a _____

     • Allowed the _____

Conclusion: The lecture and the reading differ because the reading states that _____ caused the fall of Rome, and the lecture states that _____ caused it.

Step 4

Complete the response using your outline from Step 3.

   The reading and the lecture discuss _____.
The reading says that Rome fell because _____.
The reading says that _____ made it harder to trade.
The reading also says that _____.
   The lecture says that Rome fell because _____.
In the lecture, the speaker offers two points to support his theory. The first is that

_____.

This was bad for two reasons. Commodus was _____

_____.

The second point is that one of the leaders _____.
This caused _____.
It also allowed _____.
   The reading and lecture differ because _____

_____.

Check-up

Fill in the blanks with the correct words.

valuable	spoil	cheer up	otherwise
fall	troops	loyal	invades

1. It is usually considered an act of war if a country's army _____ another country.

2. Gold is a very _____ metal.

3. In the ancient battle of Thermopylae, the Spartan king fought with only 300 _____.

4. You must study; _____, you might fail.

5. The flowers really seemed to _____ your mother.

6. Many people like to own dogs because they are such a(n) _____ pet.

7. The _____ of the city happened after it was attacked for three days.

8. If you _____ children, they will often misbehave.

[2] Independent

Getting Ready to Write

A. Learn the words.

Key Vocabulary

repay	to pay back after borrowing money
stranger	a person you do not know
feelings	a set of emotions
loan	an amount of money that is borrowed

TOEFL® Vocabulary

disrupt	to upset
nature	the qualities or characteristics of someone's personality
guilty	feeling very ashamed
hinder	to make difficult or to block
retain	to continue to have or hold

B. Read the prompt. Then answer the questions.

Describe an experience you shared with a friend recently.

1. What was the experience?
   The experience was _____.

2. Why did you do this?
   We did this because _____.

3. Did you and your friend enjoy the experience?
   We _____.

4. Do you think that money was important to this experience?
   I think that _____.

Practice

A. Read the question.

Do you agree or disagree with the following statement?

> Borrowing money from a friend can harm the relationship.

Use specific reasons and examples to support your answer.

B. Read the sample response. Then answer the question.

I think that borrowing money from a friend is not a good idea. In fact, it can be very bad. It can ruin a friendship. I think there are two reasons it can do this. First, for most people, asking to borrow money is awkward. It is even more awkward between friends. Friends are supposed to be able to talk easily to each other. But asking for a loan from a friend disrupts the relaxed nature of a friendship. It makes it hard to talk about other things. Second, borrowing money becomes a bigger problem if you can't pay it back. To borrow money means that you have to pay it back. However, if your friend needs the money and you can't repay him, you are going to feel guilty. Feeling like that can hinder communication between even the best of friends. If you want to retain your friendship, don't borrow money from your friend.

Which side of the statement does the response take?
(A) Agree   (B) Disagree

C. Complete the outline for the response.

Topic: Borrowing money from a friend _____ a good idea.
A. Asking to borrow money is _____
   1. It is even more awkward _____
   2. Asking for a loan from a friend _____
   3. Makes it hard to _____
B. Borrowing money becomes _____
   1. To borrow money means _____
   2. If you can't repay your friend, you _____
   3. Feelings like that _____
Conclusion: If you want to retain your friendship, _____
_____.

D. Underline the transitional words or phrases in the sample response.

E. Read the sample response. Then answer the question.

I think that it is fine to borrow money from a friend. Actually, it is better to take a loan from a friend than to take one from a stranger. There are two good reasons for this. First of all, friends should help each other out with their problems. For example, I would never feel guilty about asking my friend for money. That is because he knows I would do the same for him. In order to retain our friendship, we know we must be there for each other. Secondly, helping out a friend with money problems will not hinder a friendship; it can make it stronger. Friendship is about trust. If you can't trust your friends with money, then how can you trust them with your feelings? Therefore, borrowing money from a friend is a way to build trust between friends. In conclusion, these two reasons show that borrowing money from a friend is not a bad idea.

Which side of the statement does the response take?

(A) Agree   (B) Disagree

Outline

F. Complete the outline for the response.

Topic: It is _____ to borrow money from a friend.
A. Friends should help each other _____
   1. I would never feel guilty _____
   2. My friend knows _____
   3. In order to retain our friendship, _____
B. Helping out a friend with money problems _____
   1. It can make the friendship _____
   2. Friendship is about _____
   3. Borrowing money can help build _____
Conclusion: In conclusion, borrowing money from a friend _____.

G. Underline the transitional words or phrases in the sample response.

TOEFL® Vocabulary Practice

H. Fill in the blanks with the correct words.

disrupt	guilty	hinder	nature	retain

1. Many families think that it is important to _____ their traditions.
2. Natural disasters can _____ the smooth flow of an economy.
3. A person's _____, more than their abilities, shapes their attitude toward life.
4. Lack of sleep will _____ a student's ability to do well in school.
5. The boy felt _____ after he took money from his mother's purse.

Test

Step 1

Read the question.

Do you agree or disagree with the following statement?

Borrowing money from a friend can harm the relationship.

Use specific reasons and examples to support your answer.

Step 2

State your opinion.

I _____ with the statement.

Step 3

Write an outline for your essay that will support your decision.

Topic: Borrowing money from a friend _____.

A. _____

    1. _____

    2. _____

B. _____

    1. _____

    2. _____

Conclusion: _____.

Step 4

Complete the response using your outline from above.

I think that _____

_____.

First, _____.

For instance, _____

_____

_____.

Moreover, _____.

Secondly, _____.

For example, _____

_____

_____.

Therefore, I think that _____

_____.

Getting Ready to Write

A. Learn the words.

Key Vocabulary

materials	the different things used to make something
fairly	not completely; somewhat
circulate	to move something around without stopping
dirt	the soil of the ground

TOEFL® Vocabulary

alter	to change something in order to make it different
fundamental	related to the most important part of something
thus	as a result; therefore
evolve	to change slowly over a long period of time
transform	to make something completely different

Reading Passage

B. Read the first part of a passage. Then answer the questions.

Building Designs

Some builders use building designs from other countries. The designs are often altered in fundamental ways. Builders must change designs to fit the needs of a country. This often happens in two ways.

1. What is the main idea of the passage?

(A) Different types of building designs

(B) How builders change building designs

2. What do you think the rest of the passage will talk about? Write two or three ideas below.

_____

_____

Practice

A. **Listen to the first part of a lecture. Then answer the question.** `Track 5`

What is the main idea of the lecture?

(A) Reasons why churches in New Mexico changed

(B) Comparing building types in different countries

Note-taking

B. **Read the full passage. Then listen to the full lecture. Take notes in the boxes below.** `Track 6`

Building Designs

Some builders use building designs from other countries. The designs are often altered in fundamental ways. Builders must change designs to fit the needs of their own countries. This often happens in two ways.

First, building in different climates can change a design. One country may have a cold climate. Another may be in a warm place. Thus, a house in a cold place may be built to keep heat in. Builders in a warm place might want to use the same design. The design would evolve to keep heat out.

In addition, many countries must use different materials. They use the materials that are available to them. One country may have wood to build with. Another country may only have stone. The first country may have made a house with wood. A similar house in the other country would have to use stone.

Reading

Main idea: Building designs change when they are moved to another country.
Key points:

- _____ can change a building's design.
- Many countries must use _____

Lecture

Main idea: Churches in New Mexico had to transform from Spanish designs.
Key points:
- Spain and New Mexico _____
  - Spain's climate is _____, but New Mexico's can be _____
  - New Mexico churches were not _____
- The churches in New Mexico used _____
  - The Spanish churches were _____
  - The builders in New Mexico _____, so they
    built with _____

C. Read the prompt.

Summarize the main points made in the lecture and explain how they support the main points in the reading passage.

D. Fill in the blanks of the sample response using phrases from the box. Use your notes to help you.

The reading says that _____ must change when they are moved to a new country. _____ two points to support this. First, a location's climate can make builders change a design. Other times, some builders have to _____ because they have different materials to build with.

The lecture supports the reading by giving an example. The speaker discusses _____. The speaker says the designs came from Spain but changed. First, Spain and New Mexico have _____. Spain is mild, but New Mexico is sometimes very hot. Therefore, the churches in New Mexico do not have large windows. The builders in New Mexico also had to use _____. Spanish churches used stone, but the builders in New Mexico used mud.

The author offers	building designs
different materials	alter a building's design
churches in New Mexico	different climates

E. Fill in the blanks with the correct words.

alter   fundamental   thus   transform   evolve

1. The student studied very hard, and _____ she got a good grade on her test.

2. Some businesses make meetings a _____ part of their daily activities.

3. Some people _____ pieces of clothing to make them fit better.

4. Plants and animals can _____ over thousands or millions of years.

5. Many people predicted that the Internet would completely _____ the way we do business.

Test

Step 1

Read the passage. Then listen to the lecture. Take notes in the boxes below. Track 7

> ### Changing Designs
>
> Some builders like using designs from history. However, builders often change these designs. Many builders change designs to make them better and more modern. Builders do this in two ways.
>
> First, they can change designs to use new materials. Some old buildings were made with simple materials. A similar building today might use new materials. Earlier cultures would not have had these materials. Thus, the building may look similar to the old type of building. The new building would use stronger and better materials, though.
>
> In addition, some buildings change to match the modern style. The old style may have used one type of small detail. A modern builder might want to use the same building type. However, he or she might not like the way a column looked. The new builder would change that detail to match the modern style.

Reading

Main idea: Many builders change designs from history to make them more modern.
Key points:
- They can change designs to _____
- Some buildings can change designs to _____

Lecture

Main idea: Old building designs transform when they are used for modern buildings.
Key points:
- Buildings change when _____
  - Older buildings did not _____
  - Many new buildings use _____
- Some cultures have _____
  - Leaves were _____
  - When Greek buildings are made today, _____

Step 2

Read and listen to the prompt. Track 8

Summarize the main points made in the lecture and explain how they support the main points in the reading passage.

Step 3

Complete the outline using your notes from Step 1.

Topic: The changes to buildings when they are built in different countries.

A. The reading says that builders _____

   1. Builders change designs to _____

   2. Builders also change designs to _____

B. The lecture supports the reading with examples.

   1. Buildings can change when _____

     • Buildings in the past _____

     • Many new buildings _____

   2. Buildings can change when cultures _____

     • Leaves were _____

     • A modern building made in the Greek style used _____

Conclusion: Designs can change when used in a _____.

Step 4

Complete the response using your outline from Step 3.

>   The reading and the lecture discuss _____
>
> _____.
>
> The reading says _____.
>
> Builders _____.
>
> Builders also _____.
>
>   The lecture _____.
>
> First, the speaker says that buildings can change _____
>
> _____.
>
> Many new buildings _____.
>
> Second, the speaker says that buildings _____
>
> _____. For example, leaves were _____
>
> _____. A building built recently with a Greek style
>
> used _____.
>
>   In conclusion, the lecture confirms that designs _____
>
> _____.

Check-up

Fill in the blanks with the correct words.

materials	fairly	circulate	dirt
stranger	repay	feelings	loan

1. Bricks and stones were popular _____ used in many historical buildings.
2. Many students must find work to _____ their student loans.
3. A mortgage is a type of _____ used to buy a house.
4. A _____ is a person you do not know.
5. An air conditioner is a machine used to _____ cool air through a room.
6. Actors are skilled at showing many different _____.
7. Our memories are not perfect, but they are _____ good at remembering important facts.
8. When _____ is mixed with water, it becomes mud.

[03] Independent

Getting Ready to Write

A. Learn the words.

Key Vocabulary

polite	showing good manners
elder	an older person
worse	more unpleasant or bad
naughty	bad or troublesome

TOEFL® Vocabulary

obvious	easy to notice or understand
overall	considering everything; in general
modest	not proud or boastful
pretend	to act as if doing something
criticism	a statement about what is bad about something

B. Read the prompt. Then answer the questions.

Describe the characteristics of a well-behaved person.

1. Who is someone you know who is well behaved?
   That person is _____.

2. What makes them well behaved?
   That person is well behaved because _____.

3. How do you feel when you are around this person?
   I feel _____.

4. How do older people act when they are around this person?
   They act like _____.

Practice

A. Read the question.

Do you agree or disagree with the following statement?

Nowadays children do not behave as well as children once did.

Use specific reasons and examples to support your answer.

B. Read the sample response. Then answer the question.

I think that children today do not behave as well as children did in the past. There are two obvious examples of this. The first is that children are less polite today than they were before. My parents and grandparents tell me that, overall, children were more polite in the past. Almost every kid back then was more modest in public. They said things like "please" and "thank you." Today kids don't do that. The second thing is that children today don't have respect for their elders. For example, in school many of the kids in my classes don't listen to the teachers. They don't want to pay attention or listen to anything that adults say. Even worse, a few students pretend to be good but then act badly when the teacher is not looking. I don't think that kids did that as much in the past as they do now. For these reasons, I don't think kids today behave as well as children once did.

Which side of the statement does the response take?
(A) Agree   (B) Disagree

C. Complete the outline for the response.

Topic: Children today _____ as well as children did in the past.
A. Kids today _____
   1. In the past, _____
   2. Almost every kid back then _____
B. Kids no longer _____
   1. Many kids in school _____
   2. They didn't do that as much in the past _____
Conclusion: _____.

D. Underline the transitional words or phrases in the sample response.

E. Read the sample response. Then answer the question.

I think that children today behave as well as children in the past. In my opinion, children have always been naughty. It is the nature of a child to have fun and break the rules. Sometimes, this may seem like they do not respect their elders. For example, my parents say they used to pretend to listen to the teacher in school. However, they were really writing notes to friends. Obviously, that didn't stop them from punishing us when we were bad. Secondly, I don't think that kids today behave any worse than kids did before. One criticism is that there are more things to distract kids today. Kids play with video games or use cell phones when they shouldn't. However, I don't think this is bad behavior. In conclusion, I think that children do not behave any worse than children did in the past.

Which side of the statement does the response take?
(A) Agree   (B) Disagree

F. Complete the outline for the response.
Topic: Children today _____ as well as children in the past.
A. Children have _____
    1. My parents didn't listen _____
    2. They wrote _____
B. Kids today don't behave _____
    1. It is the nature of a child _____
    2. Playing with video games and cell phones _____
Conclusion: I think that children _____.

G. Underline the transitional words or phrases in the sample response.

H. Fill in the blanks with the correct words.

criticism	modest	obvious	overall	pretend

1. Although it rained for a few days, I enjoyed the vacation _____.
2. It is quite _____ that if you eat too much chocolate, you will feel ill.
3. There is nothing worse than _____ from people who you thought were your friends.
4. In the old days, women wore more _____ clothing than they do today.
5. I enjoy being in the school play because I get to _____ to be someone else.

Test

Step 1

Read the question.

Do you agree or disagree with the following statement?

Nowadays children do not behave as well as children once did.

Use specific reasons and examples to support your answer.

Step 2

State your opinion.

I _____ with the statement.

Step 3

Write an outline for your essay that will support your opinion.

Topic: Children today _____ as well as children in the past.

A. _____

    1. _____

    2. _____

B. _____

    1. _____

    2. _____

Conclusion: This is why I think that children _____

_____.

Step 4

Complete the response using your outline from above.

    I think that _____.

I think this for two reasons. First, _____

_____.

For example, _____.

In my opinion, _____

Secondly, _____

_____.

For example, _____

_____.

For these reasons, _____

_____.

Integrated - Botany

Getting Ready to Write

A. Learn the words.

cure	a medicine given to a sick person
treat	to use medicine to make a sick person better
illness	a disease; a sickness
public	people in general

facilitate	to help the progress of something
comprehensive	including many or all parts of something
medical	relating to the study or practice of medicine
transition	the process of changing from one thing to another
catalog	to make a list of a group of things

Reading Passage

B. Read the first part of a passage. Then answer the questions.

Botany

Botany is a popular science today. It first became popular in the 1800s. Yet scientists did not make it so popular. Ordinary people did. It was a hobby for them. They loved to find new plants. Just seeing the pretty flowers was fun. Then how did it become popular? A couple of things facilitated this.

1. What is the main idea of the passage?

    (A) A definition of botany

    (B) How botany became popular

2. What do you think the rest of the passage will talk about? Write two or three ideas below.

   _____

   _____

Practice

A. Listen to the first part of a lecture. Then answer the question. `Track 9`

What is the main idea of the lecture?

(A) How people studied botany

(B) Why science made botany popular

B. Read the full passage. Then listen to the full lecture. Take notes in the boxes below. `Track 10`

Botany

Botany is a popular science today. It first became popular in the 1800s. Yet scientists did not make it so popular. Ordinary people did. It was a hobby for them. They loved to find new plants. Just seeing the pretty flowers was fun. Then how did it become popular? A couple of things facilitated this.

First, people opened big gardens. Big cities often had one here and one there. People visited them in their free time. These gardens had comprehensive collections of plants. Even those who did not study botany went to these places. Many began to enjoy botany after visiting the gardens.

In addition, botany was not a complex activity. It was easy for all types of people to do. It only required a tool or two. Furthermore, lots of education was not needed. Anyone could enjoy it. Common people, not scientists, made it popular.

Reading

Main idea: Ordinary people made botany popular.
Key points:
- People _____ where ordinary people could enjoy plants.
- Botany was _____

Lecture

Main idea: Botany became popular because of science.
Key points:
- The study of plants had _____
  - Plants were _____
  - People wanted to see _____
- Lots of scientists wanted _____
  - Many of them created _____
  - The public also _____

C. Read the prompt.

Summarize the main points made in the lecture and explain how they differ from the main points in the reading passage.

D. Fill in the blanks of the sample response using phrases from the box. Use your notes to help you.

The reading says that botany became popular because of _____. The author supports this with two pieces of evidence. First, _____ people opened botanical gardens where ordinary people could go _____. Also, botany was easy for ordinary people to study because it is not a complex science.

The lecture, however, says that botany became popular because of science. The speaker believes this for two reasons. First, botany was often used in medicine. Plants were sometimes _____. Because of that, ordinary people wanted to study botany too.

In addition, the speaker says that _____ to make a list of all the plants in the world. Many of them created systems to catalog plants. After that, _____ the hunt for new plants.

the author says	scientists wanted
to enjoy plants	ordinary people
the public joined	used in cures

E. Fill in the blanks with the correct words.

facilitate   comprehensive   medical   transition   catalog

1. Surgery is a type of _____ study.
2. The telephone is a way to _____ communication between people who are apart.
3. Libraries often _____ their collections so people can find books more easily.
4. Getting a job is just one part of the _____ from childhood to adulthood.
5. A dictionary is a _____ book of the words in a language.

Test

Step 1

Read the passage. Then listen to the lecture. Take notes in the boxes below. Track 11

> **Botany**
>
> At first, botany was not a scientific study. Most people thought it was just a hobby. Its status transformed in the 1800s. It became a science. The public facilitated the change from hobby to science. This is true for two reasons.
>
> To begin, botanical gardens were meant for the public. Ordinary people went to these gardens. They went to relax and look at plants. Over time, these people began to study the plants. They wanted to learn more about them. After that, scientists became involved. They found that plant study was worthwhile.
>
> In addition, botany was not done by scientists at first. They did not like it. They thought it was not academic enough. Mostly, common people studied plants for fun. Later, scientists saw that botany did have academic uses. After this, scientists began to study botany. However, it was the public that made it an academic subject.

Reading

Main idea: The public helped botany transform from a hobby to a science.
Key points:
- Botanical gardens were _____
- Botany was not _____

Lecture

Main idea: Botany became a science when scientists became interested in it.
- Universities created _____
  - Original botanical gardens were _____
  - University botanical gardens allowed _____
    _____
- Carl Linnaeus _____
  - He created _____
  - After that, people _____

Step 2

Read and listen to the prompt. Track 12

Summarize the main points made in the lecture and explain how they differ from the main points in the reading passage.

Step 3

Complete the outline using your notes from Step 1.

Topic: The reasons why botany became a science.

A. The reading says that botany became a science because of _____
   1. Botanical gardens were places that _____
   2. At first, botany was not _____
B. The lecture says that _____
   1. Universities _____
      • Botanical gardens were _____
      • University botanical gardens _____
      _____
   2. Botany became more academic when _____
      • Carl Linnaeus _____
      • After that, people _____

Conclusion: Therefore, scientists _____.

Step 4

Complete the response using your outline from Step 3.

The reading and the lecture discuss _____.

The reading says _____.

Botanical gardens _____.

At first, botany _____.

The lecture, however, disagrees. The lecture says that _____
_____.

To begin, the speaker says that universities _____.

Botanical gardens were _____.

University botanical gardens _____
_____.

Second, the speaker says that botany _____
_____.

Carl Linnaeus _____.

After that, people _____.

In conclusion, the lecture disagrees with the reading because _____
_____
_____.

Check-up

Fill in the blanks with the correct words.

polite	elders	worse	naughty
cure	treat	illness	public

1. The flu is a(n) _____ that begins to spread in the winter each year.
2. Many people feel that children must obey their _____.
3. Surveys are used to find out what the general _____ thinks about various issues.
4. Saying "please" and "thank you" is one way of being _____.
5. Parents should punish their children for _____ behavior.
6. Doctors are people who are trained to _____ people who are sick.
7. Many scientists are searching for a(n) _____ for cancer.
8. A tornado is much _____ than a thunderstorm.

[4] Independent

Getting Ready to Write

A. Learn the words.

Key Vocabulary

value	the importance or worth of something
spirit	a sense or feeling
unite	to come together
accomplishment	a completed goal

TOEFL® Vocabulary

team	a group of people working for the same goal
point of view	an opinion; a perspective
teamwork	cooperation in a group
assist	to help
regardless	independent of; without concern for

B. Read the prompt. Then answer the questions.

Describe a group activity that you participated in recently.

1. What was the activity?
The activity was _____.

2. Who was in the group?
The group consisted of _____.

3. How did you feel about the activity?
I felt that _____.

4. Why did you participate in this group?
I participated in the group because _____.

Practice

A. Read the question.

Do you agree or disagree with the following statement?

Belonging to a group or an organization is an important part of life.

Use specific reasons and examples to support your answer.

B. Read the sample response. Then answer the question.

I think that belonging to a group or organization is not important. The main reason that I think this is that groups are mainly for people who are not independent. For example, at school some people say joining a group or a team makes you feel good. I don't agree with that point of view. I enjoy being on a team at school, but I prefer to work alone. When I work alone, I know that my accomplishments are only mine. That makes me feel good. Secondly, a lot of people join groups because they don't want to be alone. They say that everyone should experience the spirit of teamwork. However, being alone is an important part of life too. Of course, I like to spend time with my friends, but I'd rather spend most of my time alone and only unite with other people when I have to. Therefore, I think that groups are not very important.

Which side of the statement does the response take?
(A) Agree   (B) Disagree

C. Complete the outline for the response.

Topic: Belonging to a group or organization is _____.
A. Groups are mainly for people _____
    1. I don't agree that joining a group or team _____
    2. I prefer to work alone and know _____
B. A lot of people join a group because _____
    1. Being alone is _____
    2. I'd rather spend _____
Conclusion: I think that _____.

D. Underline the transitional words or phrases in the sample response.

E. Read the sample response. Then answer the question.

I think that being part of a group or organization is very important. There are two reasons for this. To begin with, I think that many people join a group to make friends. For example, I decided to join the soccer team in high school in order to meet people. I made some great friends there, many of whom I'll never forget. I also think that being part of a group allows us to achieve more than we can do on our own. Soccer taught me the value of teamwork. I used to think that only excellent soccer players scored all the goals. But when I joined the high school team, I learned that a good team must unite and everyone must assist each other to score a goal and win. Regardless of how good you are at scoring goals, it is a lot harder to do it by yourself. For these reasons, I think that groups, like a soccer team, are an important part of life.

Which side of the statement does the response take?

(A) Agree   (B) Disagree

Outline

F. Complete the outline for the response.

Topic: Being part of a group or organization _____.
A. I think that many people _____
    1. I joined the soccer team in high school _____
    2. I made _____
B. Being part of a group _____
    1. Soccer taught me _____
    2. On a team, everyone must assist each other _____
Conclusion: I think that groups, like a soccer team, _____.

G. Underline the transitional words or phrases in the sample response.

TOEFL® Vocabulary Practice

H. Fill in the blanks with the correct words.

assist	point of view	regardless	team	teamwork

1. _____ of his unfriendly appearance, he is a very kind person.
2. The group used _____ to accomplish their tasks faster than they each could alone.
3. If you can _____ me, I will be very grateful for your help.
4. When you are part of a(n) _____, you are expected to participate.
5. The man clearly did not agree with my _____ on the matter.

Test

Step 1

Read the question.

Do you agree or disagree with the following statement?

Belonging to a group or an organization is an important part of life.

Use specific reasons and examples to support your answer.

Step 2

State your opinion.

I _____ with the statement.

Step 3

Write an outline for your essay that will support your opinion.

Topic: Belonging to a group or organization _____.

A. _____

    1. _____

    2. _____

B. _____

    1. _____

    2. _____

Conclusion: _____.

Step 4

Complete the response using your outline from above.

I think that _____.

First, _____.

I say this because _____

_____

_____.

Everyone _____.

Secondly, _____.

For example, _____

_____

_____.

For these two reasons, _____.

Getting Ready to Write

A. Learn the words.

Key Vocabulary

artifact	an object that was made in ancient times
decay	to be naturally destroyed over time
fixed	not changing
flawed	having problems or lacking something important

TOEFL® Vocabulary

radiation	a form of energy caused by chemical reactions
derive	to learn something by using other information
identical	exactly the same
equation	a mathematics problem used to find a number
definite	clearly decided and unchanging

Reading Passage

B. Read the first part of a passage. Then answer the questions.

Carbon Dating

Carbon dating is used to find out the ages of many things. Scientists use it to guess how old artifacts are. It works due to carbon. Carbon is an element that is in all living things. When a plant or animal dies, its carbon radiation starts to decay. Scientists can derive age by seeing how much of its carbon has decayed. This method is very precise for two reasons.

1. What is the main idea of the passage?

   (A) Why carbon dating is precise

   (B) How carbon is used in chemistry

2. What do you think the rest of the passage will talk about? Write two or three ideas below.

   _____

   _____

Practice

A. Listen to the first part of a lecture. Then answer the question. `Track 13`

What is the main idea of the lecture?

(A) The problems of carbon dating

(B) A new method of carbon dating

Note-taking

B. Read the full passage. Then listen to the full lecture. Take notes in the boxes below. `Track 14`

Carbon Dating

Carbon dating is used to find out the ages of many things. Scientists use it to guess how old artifacts are. It works due to carbon. Carbon is an element that is in all living things. When a plant or animal dies, its carbon radiation starts to decay. Scientists can derive age by seeing how much of its carbon has decayed. This method is very precise for two reasons.

To begin, carbon decays at a fixed rate. All carbon acts in an identical way. Half of a sample of carbon will decay after 5,730 years. So if half of a plant's carbon has decayed, it is 5,730 years old.

Next, all plants and animals have the same fraction of carbon and carbon radiation. This means that the equation to find age is always the same. Also, it means that carbon dating works for all plants and animals.

Reading

Main idea: Carbon dating is a precise way to find the age of an artifact.
Key points:
- Carbon decays _____
- All plants and animals have _____

Lecture

Main idea: Carbon dating is not a very precise process.
Key points:
- Carbon has not always _____
  - Carbon decayed _____ in the past.
  - There's no way to know _____
- Carbon dating can only date _____
  - If it is older than that, there's _____
  - It is a technique that can't _____

C. Read the prompt.

Summarize the main points made in the lecture and explain how they differ from the main points in the reading passage.

D. Fill in the blanks of the sample response using phrases from the box. Use your notes to help you.

The reading says that carbon dating is a precise way to find the _____. The author supports this with two points. First, _____ at a fixed rate. The author also says that all plants and animals have the same fraction of carbon and carbon radiation.

The lecture, on the other hand, says that carbon dating is not precise. _____ two pieces of evidence to support this viewpoint. The speaker says that carbon has not always decayed _____. Carbon decayed much more quickly in the past. There's no way we can know exactly how it decayed in the past. Also, carbon dating can only _____ that are less than 40,000 years old. If the object is older than that, there is _____ carbon left. Therefore, it is a technique that can't be used in all situations.

date objects	carbon decays
not enough	the speaker gives
age of artifacts	at the same rate

E. Fill in the blanks with the correct words.

radiation	derive	identical	equation	definite

1. The sun sends out _____ in the form of ultraviolet rays.

2. To find the length of a triangle's side, you must use a(n) _____ called the Pythagorean theorem.

3. The stock market crash of 1929 caused a(n) _____ change in how people spent money.

4. Doctors can _____ a patient's diagnosis by studying their symptoms.

5. Words that have _____ spellings but mean different things are called homonyms.

Test

Step 1

Carbon Dating

Many people think we need to improve the carbon dating process. At this point, the process is flawed. It is hard to find definite dates of things. However, there are two things that can be done to make carbon dating better.

First, scientists need to calibrate their results. The rate at which carbon decays has changed over the years. Calibration uses other living things to find past rates of decay. For example, trees are often used. Scientists can look at tree rings to find a tree's age. They can use carbon dating to find the carbon level through the tree's life. This tells them how fast carbon decayed at certain times.

Second, scientists must remove chemicals from items. Some chemicals can change the results of dating. They put out radiation that mixes with the carbon. However, scientists can use other chemicals to remove the bad ones. The new chemicals do not affect the dating. These two things can make carbon dating a good way to date objects.

Reading

Main idea: There are two ways that carbon dating can be improved.
Key points:
- Scientists need to _____
- Scientists must remove _____

Lecture

Main idea: The two possible solutions to carbon dating problems won't work.
Key points:
- Using _____ to make dating more precise won't work.
  - Not many trees have _____
  - One tree can only be used _____
- Using chemicals makes dating _____
  - Some scientists use _____
  - These chemicals can _____

Step 2

Summarize the main points made in the lecture and explain how they differ from the main points in the reading passage.

Step 3

Complete the outline using your notes from Step 1.

Topic: How carbon dating can be improved.

A. The reading says that there are _____

    1. Scientists need to _____

    2. Scientists must _____

B. The lecture says that _____

    1. Using tree rings _____

      • Not many trees have _____

      • One tree can only be used _____

    2. Using chemicals makes _____

      • Some scientists _____

      • These chemicals _____

Conclusion: Therefore, these two ideas _____.

Step 4

Complete the response using your outline from Step 3.

    The reading and the lecture discuss _____
_____.

The reading says _____.

Scientists need _____.

In addition, they must _____
_____.

    The lecture challenges what is said in the reading. The speaker says that _____
_____.

To begin, the speaker says that _____
_____.

Not many trees _____.

Also, one tree can only be used _____.

Second, the speaker says that using chemicals _____.

Some scientists _____.

However, these chemicals _____.

    In conclusion, the lecture challenges the reading because _____
_____.

Check-up

Fill in the blanks with the correct words.

value	spirit	unite	accomplishment
artifact	decay	fixed	flawed

1. Most companies will not sell a product if it is _____ in even a small way.

2. When a research team finds a(n) _____, it is first studied and then it is sometimes displayed in a museum.

3. The spread of the Internet has shown the _____ of information.

4. After a plant dies, its leaves will quickly begin to _____.

5. When you _____ hydrogen and oxygen, you can make water.

6. Some people think that night games in baseball go against the _____ of the game.

7. Being accepted to Harvard is a great _____.

8. Many businesses allow you to pay a(n) _____ amount of money each month for an expensive product.

[5] Independent

Getting Ready to Write

A. Learn the words.

Key Vocabulary

volunteer	to do something without payment
rebel	to go against something
free time	a time not spent working
similarly	likewise

TOEFL® Vocabulary

regard	to consider
engage	to become involved in an activity
integrate	to bring together or combine
relevant	meaningful or interesting
fulfill	to meet a goal or complete something

B. Read the prompt. Then answer the questions.

Describe something you have done with your community.

1. What did you do?

I took part in _____.

2. Who did you do it with?

I did it with _____.

3. Why did you do it?

I did it because _____.

4. What did you think about the experience?

I think that _____.

Practice

A. Read the question.

Do you agree or disagree with the following statement?

All young people should spend a few hours a month working to help their community.

Use specific reasons and examples to support your answer.

B. Read the sample response. Then answer the question.

Young people should help in their communities. I think this is very important. If they can do it every month, it is even better. I feel this way for two reasons. First, I think that volunteering teaches young people responsibility. Some young people rebel against their community. However, when they work for it, they learn about its problems. They also learn how they can help solve a problem. Young people can solve problems. Nearly everyone regards this as good. Second, volunteering engages young people. They become active in their communities. Too often people do not know their own neighbors. However, when they work to help their community, they meet people that they didn't even know were there. Meeting new people is fun. They might even make a few new friends. Furthermore, knowing people in the community helps a kid to better integrate into it. Young people must help out in their areas. This is very important. The benefits are relevant to everyone.

Which side of the statement does the response take?
(A) Agree   (B) Disagree

C. Complete the outline for the response.

Topic: It is important for _____.
A. Volunteering teaches _____
   1. When they work for their community, _____
   2. They also learn _____
B. Volunteering _____ in their communities.
   1. When they work to help their community, _____
   2. Knowing people in the community _____
Conclusion: Young people must help out in their areas because the benefits _____
_____.

D. Underline the transitional words or phrases in the sample response.

E. Read the sample response. Then answer the question.

I don't think that young people should have to spend time working to help their communities. There are two reasons for this. The first one is that young people will spend the rest of their lives working. When you are young, it is the only time you have to play. Even then, most young people have busy schedules. Their free time is theirs alone and they should use it to have fun while they are still young. Kids should play! Next, kids must make money when they work. Usually, when you work to help your community, you do it as a volunteer. My dad says that it is never a good idea to work without getting paid. That makes sense to me. It shows that you do not regard your time as having any value. Similarly, you should always get a reward when you fulfill your responsibilities. If you work for free, you do not get any relevant rewards. So, for these reasons, I think that young people should not have to work to help their communities. They have the rest of their lives to do that and they can get paid for it as adults too.

Which side of the statement does the response take?

(A) Agree (B) Disagree

Outline

F. Complete the outline for the response.

Topic: Young people should not _____.
A. Young people will spend _____
   1. When you are young, _____
   2. Their free time is theirs alone, and they should _____
B. Kids must _____
   1. Usually, when you work to help your community, _____
   2. You should always get a reward _____
Conclusion: I think that young people should _____.

G. Underline the transitional words or phrases in the sample response.

TOEFL® Vocabulary Practice

H. Fill in the blanks with the correct words.

engage	fulfill	integrate	regard	relevant

1. Many people _____ Christmas as the most joyous holiday of the year.
2. New students often find it hard to _____ into a new school.
3. Clearly, typewriters are not _____ to businesses like they once were.
4. More people should _____ in regular exercise and fitness activities.
5. I _____ my obligation to my church by helping to feed homeless people.

Test

Step 1

Read the question.

Do you agree or disagree with the following statement?

All young people should spend a few hours a month working to help their community.

Use specific reasons and examples to support your answer

Step 2

State your opinion.

I _____ with the statement.

Step 3

Write an outline for your essay that will support your opinion.

Topic: Young people _____ volunteer to help their communities.

A. _____

   1. _____

   2. _____

B. _____

   1. _____

   2. _____

Conclusion: For these reasons, I think that young people _____

_____.

Step 4

Complete the response using your outline from above.

I think that _____.

First, _____.

Furthermore, _____

_____

_____.

Second, _____.

For example, _____

_____.

In addition, _____.

In conclusion, _____

_____.

Getting Ready to Write

A. Learn the words.

Key Vocabulary

run	to manage a business
theme park	a large area where people go to play games and go on rides
control	to keep something at the correct level
ride	a machine that people go in to have fun

TOEFL® Vocabulary

merchant	a person or business that sells products
generate	to make
revenue	the money that a business makes
adjustment	a change to make something better
objective	a goal that a person or business has

Reading Passage

B. Read the first part of a passage. Then answer the questions.

Seasonal Businesses

Some merchants are only open in one season. They run seasonal businesses. There are many kinds of seasonal merchants. Some are open only in the summer when the weather is good. Others are only open in the winter when there is snow. This can make it hard to run a business. But many think this type of business is a good idea. There are two things that help seasonal merchants do well.

1. What is the main idea of the passage?

(A) The types of seasonal businesses

(B) How to run a seasonal business well

2. What do you think the rest of the passage will talk about? Write two or three ideas below.

_____

_____

Practice

A. Listen to the first part of a lecture. Then answer the question. Track 17

What is the main idea of the lecture?

(A) How seasonal businesses adjust to closing

(B) Why seasonal businesses close at some times

B. Read the full passage. Then listen to the full lecture. Take notes in the boxes below. Track 18

Seasonal Businesses

Some merchants are only open for one season. They run seasonal businesses. There are many kinds of seasonal merchants. Some are open only in the summer when the weather is good. Others are only open in the winter when there is snow. This can make it hard to run a business. But many think this type of business is a good idea. There are two things that help seasonal merchants do well.

First, a merchant must generate a great deal of revenue when it is open. Some merchants are only open for a few months. They must make enough money to last the whole year.

In addition, seasonal merchants must plan ahead. They must first know how much money they make. They have to plan to save money. Merchants must pay for things all year. They don't make money all year, though. This means they must control how much they spend. They can't spend too much money when they are open. If they do, they won't have money to pay for things when they are closed.

Reading

Main idea: Two things can help a seasonal business succeed.
Key points:
- A merchant must _____
- Seasonal merchants _____

Lecture

Main idea: A theme park makes enough money to close in the winter.
Key points:
- _____ is the main objective.
  - The owners try _____
  - They sell enough _____
- They have to _____
  - The park must pay to _____
  - The park also has to _____ even when it's closed.

C. Read the prompt.

Summarize the main points made in the lecture and explain how they support the main points in the reading passage.

D. Fill in the blanks of the sample response using phrases from the box. Use your notes to help you.

The reading says that seasonal businesses can be difficult _____. The author suggests two things that seasonal business owners can do. First, the business must generate _____. In addition, the owners must plan ahead.

The lecture supports the reading by _____ as an example. The speaker discusses two things that the theme park does. First, the speaker says that making money is the main objective. The owners try not to spend too much money when the park is open. They also make a lot of money by _____. In addition, _____ have to plan ahead. They sometimes have to pay to repair rides. They also have to pay taxes even when _____.

the owners	to run
using a theme park	selling tickets
the park is closed	a lot of revenue

E. Fill in the blanks with the correct words.

merchant   generate   revenue   adjustment   objective

1. Advertising is a great way to help a business _____ more money.
2. The _____ of most traffic laws is to keep drivers safe.
3. A(n) _____ must not only sell products but buy many products as well.
4. Much of the _____ that a business makes is spent paying workers.
5. Some businesses have found that a minor _____ in spending can have major effects.

Test

Step 1

Read the passage. Then listen to the lecture. Take notes in the boxes below. Track 19

> ### Seasonal Businesses
>
> Running a seasonal business can be hard for many people. It can be hard to make enough money to last the whole year. Some merchants find ways to make money when business is slow. There are two ways that a merchant can do this.
>
> Some business owners own more than one store. Each store can make money during a different part of the year. That way, the owners don't lose money during a period of the year. This makes running both stores easier.
>
> Business owners sometimes also have to add to their stores. A store might sell a product that does not sell during one season. In order to keep making money, they may have to start selling new things. The owners can sell a new product that will sell during their slow season. They would then make money all year.

Reading

Main idea: Seasonal merchants must find ways to make money when business is slow.
Key points:
- Some business owners own _____
- Business owners sometimes have to _____

Lecture

Main idea: Seasonal businesses can succeed by trying new things.
Key points:
- One seasonal business did well by _____
    - At first, the owner _____
    - Because business was bad in the winter, she _____
      _____

- A second seasonal merchant succeeded by _____
    - The store sold _____
    - She began to sell _____
      _____

Step 2

Read and listen to the prompt. Track 20

Summarize the main points made in the lecture and explain how they support the main points in the reading passage.

Step 3

Complete the outline using your notes from Step 1.

Topic: How seasonal businesses can make money when business is slow.

A. There are two ways that _____

    1. To begin, some _____

    2. Also, business owners _____

B. The lecture _____

    1. One seasonal business _____

       • At first, _____

       • Because _____,

         the business owner _____

    2. Another seasonal merchant _____

       • The store _____

       • The owner began _____

       _____

Conclusion: The lecture _____ the reading by _____

_____.

Step 4

Complete the response using your outline from Step 3.

The reading and the lecture discuss _____

_____.

The reading mentions _____.

To begin, _____.

Also, _____.

   The lecture _____.

One seasonal business _____.

At first, _____.

Because _____

_____.

Another seasonal merchant _____.

The store _____.

The owner began _____

_____.

   In conclusion, the lecture _____

_____.

Check-up

Fill in the blanks with the correct words.

volunteer	rebel	free time	similarly
theme park	run	control	ride

1. Teenagers sometimes _____ against teachers and parents.
2. Paying for repairs is one of the many costs of owning a _____.
3. Freezing weather can be unpleasant in the winter. _____, it can be unpleasant if it is too hot in the summer.
4. Many charity groups need their workers to _____ their time and energy.
5. Many people make a budget to _____ how much money they spend.
6. Many people take up hobbies in their _____.
7. A roller coaster is a popular type of _____.
8. Many new business owners choose to _____ their businesses with close friends.

[6] Independent

Getting Ready to Write

A. Learn the words.

roam	to walk around freely
threatened	likely to be harmed or destroyed
endangered	in danger of disappearing
importance	the quality of being important

population	the number of people or animals living in a particular area
decade	a ten-year period
conservation	the protection of natural things
domestic	not wild
eliminate	to get rid of

B. Read the prompt. Then answer the questions.

Describe a time you visited a zoo.

1. What did you see there?

I saw _____.

2. Why did you visit the zoo?

I went there because _____.

3. What did you like best about the experience?

I liked _____.

4. What didn't you like about the experience?

I didn't like _____.

Practice

A. Read the question.

Do you agree or disagree with the following statement?

> A zoo has no useful purpose.

Use specific reasons and examples to support your answer.

B. Read the sample response. Then answer the question.

Zoos are useful. In fact, they are very important. I feel this way for two reasons. First, zoos protect threatened animals. Some animal populations cannot survive alone. There are very few of these animals. Also, people hunt them. Some hunted animals are endangered. They may disappear in a decade. Zoos can save them. Zoos give them a safe home. There is another reason zoos are useful. They teach people about nature. Mainly, they teach people about conservation. It is sad that many people in cities do not care about nature. This is because they do not know nature. However, zoos can teach people about the importance of nature. They can teach people about respecting and protecting all the plants and animals on the Earth. In conclusion, I think zoos are useful. They save the lives of endangered animals. They also teach people to conserve nature.

Which side of the statement does the response take?
(A) Agree   (B) Disagree

C. Complete the outline for the response.

Topic: Zoos are _____ and _____.
A. Zoos protect _____
    1. Some animal populations _____
    2. Zoos give them _____
B. Zoos teach people _____
    1. Zoos can teach people in cities _____
    2. They can teach people about _____
    _____

Conclusion: Zoos are _____
_____.

D. Underline the transitional words or phrases in the sample response.

E. Read the sample response. Then answer the question.

I think that zoos are not useful. In fact, I'm not sure what purpose they have. There are two main reasons I feel this way. One is that zoos are expensive. Caring for a large population of animals from around the world is expensive. If people want to care for animals, they can spend a lot less money and protect the domestic animals that live in their communities. In my community, for example, there are lots of pets that people do not take care of. Second, zoos do not teach people to respect nature. Actually, they teach people not to respect nature. If education is your goal, it is better to let animals be free and roam in nature. That is more useful than a zoo. To conclude, I don't think that zoos are useful. Rather, they are expensive and teach people to disrespect nature. We should eliminate them.

Which side of the statement does the response take?

(A) Agree   (B) Disagree

Outline

F. Complete the outline for the response.

Topic: Zoos are _____.
A. Zoos are _____
    1. Caring for a large population of animals _____
    2. It is less expensive to protect _____
B. Zoos do not teach people _____
    1. They teach people _____
    2. It is better to _____
Conclusion: Zoos are _____.

G. Underline the transitional words or phrases in the sample response.

TOEFL® Vocabulary Practice

H. Fill in the blanks with the correct words.

conservation	decade	domestic	eliminate	population

1. The _____ of the world is growing very fast.

2. Most farms have a few _____ animals like sheep, pigs, and cows.

3. We have seen many changes in this city over the last _____.

4. A good gardener must _____ all the weeds in his garden.

5. As cities grow, _____ of trees is more important than ever before.

Test

Step 1

Read the question.

Do you agree or disagree with the following statement?

A zoo has no useful purpose.

Use specific reasons and examples to support your answer.

Step 2

State your opinion.

I _____ with the statement.

Step 3

Write an outline for your essay that will support your opinion.

Topic: Zoos are _____.

A. _____

    1. _____

    2. _____

B. _____

    1. _____

    2. _____

Conclusion: _____.

Step 4

Complete the response using your outline from above.

I think _____.

First, _____.

I think _____.

Also, _____

_____.

Second, _____

_____.

I feel that _____.

In addition, _____

_____.

In conclusion, _____.

Integrated - Geology

Getting Ready to Write

A. Learn the words.

Key Vocabulary

plate	a layer of rock that forms a part of the surface of the Earth
tectonic	relating to the movement of the Earth's surface
crust	the thick outer layer of the Earth
discovery	an act of finding something for the first time

TOEFL® Vocabulary

complement	to go together well
visible	able to be seen
preliminary	coming before something else
contradict	to deny or state the opposite of something
amendment	a change or addition made to something

Reading Passage

B. Read the first part of a passage. Then answer the questions.

Plate Tectonics

Scientists in the early 20th century began to study the continents. They noticed that the continents' edges seemed to complement each other. It is that idea that led to the theory of plate tectonics. The theory says that the continents move on plates. The Earth began as one big continent. Over time, it broke apart into new, smaller continents. This idea was first made by Alfred Wegener. Many did not believe his theory at first. There were two problems with his idea.

1. What is the main idea of the passage?
(A) Problems with Wegener's theory
(B) How continents move

2. What do you think the rest of the passage will talk about? Write two or three ideas below.

_____

_____

Practice

A. Listen to the first part of a lecture. Then answer the question. `Track 21`

What is the main idea of the lecture?

(A) How Wegener's theory was changed

(B) How plate movement affects the Earth

B. Read the full passage. Then listen to the full lecture. Take notes in the boxes below. `Track 22`

Plate Tectonics

Scientists in the early 20th century began to study the continents. They noticed that the continents' edges seemed to complement each other. It is that idea that led to the theory of plate tectonics. The theory says that the continents move on plates. The Earth began as one big continent. Over time, it broke apart into new, smaller continents. This idea was first suggested by Alfred Wegener. Many did not believe his theory at first. There were two problems with his idea.

First, he could not say why the continents moved. No one could figure out what caused them to move. And there was no visible proof that they did move. Without that, many people said the theory could not be proven.

Second, many people did not think it was possible for plates to move. Wegener thought the plates moved through the ocean's crust. Many people said this was not possible. The ocean's crust was too strong to let this happen.

Reading

Main idea: There were two problems with Wegener's theory of plate tectonics.
Key points:
- Wegener could not say _____
- Many people did not think _____

Lecture

Main idea: Two major changes solved the problems of Wegener's theory.
Key points:
- The first solved the problem of _____
  - Plates move because of _____
  - The heat from the Earth's core _____
- People thought the crust was _____
  - Plates actually move _____
  - The hard part of the crust _____

C. Read the prompt.

Summarize the main points made in the lecture and explain how they differ from the main points in the reading passage.

D. Fill in the blanks of the sample response using phrases from the box. Use your notes to help you.

The reading says that there were two problems with _____ of plate tectonics. _____ the two problems. First, Wegener could not explain why the plates moved. In addition, many scientists did not think that plates could move through the thick crust.

The lecture differs from the reading because it explains how those problems were solved. The speaker says that two _____ fixed the problems with Wegener's theory. First, scientists discovered _____. Plates move because of heat from the Earth's core. Heat _____ the plates and makes them move. Second, the author says that people thought that the crust was too thick for plates to move through. Plates actually move on top of _____. The hard part of the crust moves on top of a soft part of the crust.

The author describes	why the plates move
the crust	Wegener's theory
major amendments	pushes on

E. Fill in the blanks with the correct words.

complement   visible   preliminary   contradict   amendment

1. From Earth, the stars are only _____ at night.
2. Some laws can be changed slightly by adding a(n) _____.
3. Many cooks add spices that _____ their food to make a better taste.
4. When two people disagree about an issue, their views may _____ each other.
5. While the _____ version of an essay may have problems, they can be fixed in later versions.

Test

Step 1

Read the passage. Then listen to the lecture. Take notes in the boxes below. Track 23

Pangaea

Scientists think the Earth used to be one big continent. They have given this continent the name of Pangaea. Millions of years ago, it began to break up. The movements made the continents we have today. In the future, they might come together once again. The new ones would not form one large mass of land. However, there would be two major changes.

First, Asia and Africa would join. Africa's plate will move to the northeast. Asia's plates will also move in the same way. Yet Africa's plate moves more quickly than Asia's. Thus, it will collide with Asia.

Second, North and South America will move west. This will make the Atlantic Ocean much larger. North America will also move slightly to the north. This will make the two farther apart. It will also make North America closer to the east side of Asia.

Reading

Main idea: In the future, the continents will go through two major changes.
Key points:
- Asia and Africa _____
- North and South America _____

Lecture

Main idea: The continents will form another huge continent called Pangaea Ultima.
Key points:
- Africa will _____
  - Africa will move from _____ to _____
  - It will _____ to make one continent.
- South America will _____
  - The continent will hit _____
  - The tail of the continent will _____

Step 2

Read and listen to the prompt. Track 24

Summarize the main points made in the lecture and explain how they differ from the main points in the reading passage.

Step 3

Complete the outline using your notes from Step 1.

Topic: How the continents will move in the future.

A. The reading says that they will _____

    1. To begin, _____

    2. In addition, _____

B. The lecture, on the other hand, _____

_____

    1. First, Africa will _____

        • It will move _____

        • It will _____

    2. Also, South America will _____

        • The continent will _____

        • The tail of the continent _____

Conclusion: The lecture says that _____

              instead of _____.

Step 4

Complete the sample response using your outline from Step 3.

The reading and the lecture are about _____

_____.

The reading says _____.

To begin, _____.

In addition, _____.

The lecture, on the other hand, _____

_____.

First, Africa will _____.

It will move _____.

It will _____.

Also, South America will _____.

The continent will _____.

The tail of the continent _____.

In conclusion, the lecture disagrees with the reading because the lecture says

_____

_____.

Check-up

Fill in the blanks with the correct words.

roam	threatened	tectonic	importance
plate	endangered	crust	discovery

1. The World Wildlife Fund works to protect _____ animals.

2. Scientists are only now beginning to understand the _____ of global warming.

3. Some would say that electricity is the most important _____ in history.

4. Even though Europe and Asia are considered different continents, they share the same _____.

5. Much of the world's oil must be found deep below the Earth's _____.

6. Every year, people in Kansas are _____ by seasonal tornadoes.

7. Many people believe animals should _____ free instead of being kept in zoos.

8. The movement of the surface of the Earth is called _____ movement.

[Review 1]

Step 1

Read the question.

Do you agree or disagree with the following statement?

American TV is better than Asian TV.

Use specific reasons and examples to support your answer.

Step 2

State your opinion.

I _____ with the statement.

Step 3

Write an outline for your essay that will support your opinion.

Topic: American TV is _____ Asian TV.

A. _____

   1. _____

   2. _____

B. _____

   1. _____

   2. _____

Conclusion: This is why American TV _____.

Step 4

Complete the response using your outline from above.

I think that American TV _____ Asian TV.

I think this because _____.

I think _____.

For example, _____.

Also, I think that _____.

I feel that _____.

I think this because _____.

In conclusion, this is why American TV _____.

Step 1

Read the passage. Then listen to the lecture. Take notes in the boxes below. Track 25

Nastic Movements

It's hard to believe that plants in nature can move on their own. However, many plants can do this. One type of plant movement is called a nastic movement. This type of movement happens when an external force disrupts a plant. There are two important types of nastic movements.

The first is called hyponasty. This happens when a plant moves because it is touched. Such plants move in many ways. Some make their leaves move. Other movements affect the whole plant.

The second movement is called thermonasty. These movements happen because of temperature changes. Some plants do this to protect themselves from heat or cold. Some flowers can open or close if the temperature changes. Other times, the stems of plants can change shape.

Reading

Main idea: A nastic movement happens when _____

_____

Key points:
- Hyponasty occurs when a plant moves because _____
- Thermonasty happens because of _____

Lecture

Main idea: There are two plants that _____
Key points:
- One plant that uses nastic movement is called the _____
  - It is an example of _____
  - The plant closes when an insect _____
- Another plant that demonstrates nastic movement is the _____
  - This plant uses a movement called _____

  _____
  - The plant's leaves can _____ if the temperature changes.

Step 2

Read and listen to the prompt. Track 26

Summarize the main points made in the lecture and explain how they support the main points in the reading passage.

Step 3

Topic: The reading and the lecture discuss nastic movements in plants.

A. The reading discusses two types of _____ and says how they happen.

　　1. The first type is called _____, and it happens when _____

　　　_____

　　2. The second type is called _____, which is _____

　　　_____

B. The lecture _____ by discussing two examples of nastic movements in nature.

　　1. The _____ is a plant that uses nastic movements.

　　　• Its movement is a type _____

　　　• The plant closes when _____

　　2. Another type of plant that uses nastic movements is called the _____

　　　• The plant uses a kind of movement called _____

　　　_____

　　　• If the temperature around the plant changes, its leaves _____

　　　_____

Conclusion: Therefore, the lecture _____ the reading by

_____.

Step 4

　　The reading and the lecture both discuss _____.
The reading begins by discussing _____.
The first type mentioned is called _____, and it happens when

_____.
The second type the author mentions is _____, which _____
_____.
　　The lecture _____ by discussing _____
_____.
The speaker discusses the _____, a plant that uses nastic movements.
This plant's movement is an example of _____ because it _____
_____.
The plant closes when _____.
The speaker also discusses a plant called the _____. This plant
uses a type of nastic movement called _____, which is _____
_____. If the _____ around the plant changes, its leaves

_____.
　　In conclusion, the lecture _____
_____.

Step 1

Read the passage. Then listen to the lecture. Take notes in the boxes below. `Track 27`

> ### Atlantis
>
> The Greek writer Plato wrote about a place called Atlantis. He said it sunk into the ocean many years ago. For years, no one knew if this was true. Even today, people still have many points of view on the topic. There is some definite proof that says it did exist. There are two things that support this idea.
>
> First, there are remains of Atlantis at the bottom of the ocean. Many relics have been found in the area. In addition, pieces of land have been found at the bottom of the sea. Thus, some sort of city fell into the sea. This city must have been Atlantis.
>
> Also, we can see parts of Atlantis above the water. Many think that some islands today used to be part of Atlantis. Both Bermuda and the Bahamas used to be part of Atlantis. These two areas are located in the Atlantic Ocean. They broke off from Atlantis when it sunk into the ocean.

Reading

Main idea: There is proof that _____
Key points:
- Some evidence of Atlantis has been found _____
- The remains of Atlantis can also be seen _____

Lecture

Main idea: There is nothing to suggest that _____
Key points:
- There's no evidence _____ that suggests Atlantis existed.
  - If a continent fell into the ocean, there would be _____
  - However, scientists have only found _____
- There's no reason to think that _____ used to be part of Atlantis.
  - There's nothing to suggest that they _____
  - We would have to find _____ before we could say that.

Step 2

Read and listen to the prompt. `Track 28`

Summarize the main points made in the lecture and explain how they cast doubt on the main points in the reading passage.

Step 3

Complete the outline using your notes from Step 1.

Topic: The reading and the lecture discuss whether a place called Atlantis ever existed.
A. The reading suggests that Atlantis _____
   1. Some evidence of Atlantis has been found _____
   2. The remains of Atlantis can also be seen _____
B. The lecture _____ with two points.
   1. There's no evidence _____
      • If a continent fell into the ocean, _____
      • However, scientists have _____
   2. There's no reason to think that _____
      • No evidence suggests that _____
      • For this to be true, we would have to find _____
Conclusion: The lecture _____ the reading.

Step 4

Complete the response using your outline from Step 3.

   The reading and the lecture discuss _____.
The reading begins by suggesting that _____.
First, the author says that some evidence of Atlantis _____
_____.
In addition, the author says that the remains of Atlantis _____
_____.
   The lecture _____
by stating that _____.
The speaker first says that there's no evidence _____
_____. He says that if a continent fell into the ocean, then _____
_____.
However, scientists have _____.
The speaker also says that there's no reason to think that _____
_____.
No evidence suggests that _____.
For this to be true, we would have to find _____.
   In conclusion, the lecture _____
_____.

Step 1

Read the question.

Do you agree or disagree with the following statement?

Parents should not let their children play outside without an adult.

Use specific reasons and examples to support your answer.

Step 2

State your opinion.

I _____ with the statement.

Step 3

Write an outline for your essay that will support your opinion.

Topic: Parents _____ play outside without an adult.

A. _____

    1. _____

    2. _____

B. _____

    1. _____

    2. _____

Conclusion: For these reasons, I think that _____

_____.

Step 4

Complete the response using your outline from above.

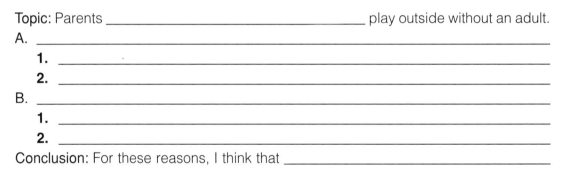

    I think that parents _____.

To begin, I think _____.

I think this because _____.

For example, _____.

Secondly, I believe _____.

This is because _____.

For example, _____.

For these reasons, I think _____

_____.

[07] Independent

Getting Ready to Write

A. Learn the words.

Key Vocabulary

lung	the organ used for breathing
second-hand smoke	smoke released into the air when a cigarette burns
non-smoker	a person who doesn't smoke
cancer	a kind of disease

TOEFL® Vocabulary

alike	the same
statistic	a numerical fact or data
deprived	lacking something
favor	a helpful act
mainstream	most common or normal

B. Read the prompt. Then answer the questions.

Describe an experience when you were around someone smoking.

1. What was the experience?
   The experience was _____.

2. How did you feel?
   I felt _____.

3. What did you do?
   I _____.

4. What do you think about smoking?
   I think that _____.

Practice

A. Read the question.

Do you agree or disagree with the following statement?

Smoking should be banned in public places.

Use specific reasons and examples to support your answer.

B. Read the sample response. Then answer the question.

I think that smoking should be banned in public. There are two reasons that I think this is the case. First, smoking is not only bad for the smoker, but it also harms other people. Smoking causes cancer in smokers and non-smokers alike. Statistics show that second-hand smoke in public places deprives non-smokers of clean, healthy air. It also increases their chances of getting lung cancer. Second, smoking in public places sets a bad example for children. Clearly, what children see around them influences their behavior. They can learn good habits or bad habits, like smoking. We are not doing children a favor when we smoke around them. Therefore, it is a good idea to ban smoking in public places to protect the health of non-smokers and to set a good example for children.

Which side of the statement does the response take?
(A) Agree (B) Disagree

C. Complete the outline for the response.

Topic: Smoking _____ banned in public.
A. Smoking is _____, but it also _____
   1. Smoking causes cancer _____
   2. Second-hand smoke deprives _____
B. Smoking in public places _____
   1. What children see around them _____
   2. They can learn good habits or _____
Conclusion: It is a good idea to _____ to protect the health
     of non-smokers and to set a good example for children.

D. Underline the transitional words or phrases in the sample response.

E. Read the sample response. Then answer the question.

I think that smoking should not be banned in public. It is a bad idea for two reasons. First, people have the right to smoke. They can smoke, just as they can eat fast food. People have the freedom to do both of these things. However, both of these activities are harmful to a person's health, yet people do them anyway. Therefore, banning smoking deprives people of their freedom to smoke. Whatever bothers the mainstream culture should not just be banned. Will banning chewing gum in public be next? Second, if non-smokers don't like smoke, they can go to other public places. It's not necessary to ban smoking in all public places. For instance, don't go to a nightclub if you don't like being around smoke. Non-smokers can go to other places to relax, like a bookstore. They can also choose whether they want to go places where people smoke. Banning smoking from all public places is ridiculous since non-smokers already have plenty of choices. In conclusion, it is not necessary to ban smoking from public places.

Which side of the statement does the response take?

(A) Agree   (B) Disagree

Outline

F. Complete the outline for the response.

Topic: Smoking _____ banned in public.
A. People have _____
   1. They _____ do things that harm them.
   2. Banning smoking deprives people _____
B. If non-smokers don't like smoke, _____
   1. Don't go to a nightclub if _____
   2. Non-smokers can _____
Conclusion: It is not necessary _____.

G. Underline the transitional words or phrases in the sample response.

TOEFL® Vocabulary Practice

H. Fill in the blanks with the correct words.

alike	deprived	favor	mainstream	statistics

1. If you do a(n) _____ for someone, that person should be thankful.
2. The government gathered _____ on population movement to cities.
3. People always say my brother and I look _____, but I do not think so.
4. A person _____ of food will soon become ill and die.
5. Many teenagers rebel against _____ culture by trying to be different.

Test

Step 1

Read the question.

Do you agree or disagree with the following statement?

Smoking should be banned in public places.

Use specific reasons and examples to support your answer.

Step 2

State your opinion.

I _____ with the statement.

Step 3

Write an outline for your essay that will support your decision.

Topic: I _____ smoking should be banned in public places.
A. _____
    1. _____
    2. _____
B. _____
    1. _____
    2. _____
Conclusion: I think _____.

Step 4

Complete the response using your outline from above.

    In my opinion, _____.
I think this _____.
First, _____.
Furthermore, _____
_____
_____.
Second, _____.
Also, _____.
In addition, _____
_____.
Therefore, _____.

Integrated - Literature

Getting Ready to Write

A. Learn the words.

Key Vocabulary

myth	an ancient story told for many years
quest	a long and difficult journey or search
hero	a main character that does good and brave things
royalty	a class of people related to kings or queens

TOEFL® Vocabulary

legend	a story in history that is not completely true
plot	a group of events in a story
evident	easy to see
tragedy	a very sad event
motive	the reason that someone does something

Reading Passage

B. Read the first part of a passage. Then answer the questions.

Science Fiction and Myths

Science fiction and ancient myths have much in common. Many of today's science fiction stories were inspired by myths. One person who studied myths and legends is Joseph Campbell. He said that myths and science fiction have two things in common.

1. What is the main idea of the passage?

   (A) Similarities of myths and science fiction

   (B) The two types of science fiction stories

2. What do you think the rest of the passage will talk about? Write two or three ideas below.

   _____

   _____

Practice

A. Listen to the first part of a lecture. Then answer the question. `Track 29`

What is the main idea of the lecture?

(A) How *Star Wars* influenced other myths

(B) How myths are similar to *Star Wars*

B. Read the full passage. Then listen to the full lecture. Take notes in the boxes below. `Track 30`

> ### Science Fiction and Myths
>
> Science fiction and ancient myths have much in common. Many of today's science fiction stories were inspired by myths. One person who studied myths and legends is Joseph Campbell. He said that myths and science fiction have two things in common.
>
> To begin, he said the characters are very similar to people in myths. He described them as "archetypes." An archetype is a model of a person. Such models are copied by many different people. They were first used in ancient myths. Science fiction stories today use the same archetypes. Thus, the characters are very similar.
>
> In addition, the plots of myths and science fiction stories are similar. This is evident in many modern plots. Most myths involve a quest. The people in the story must leave their homes. They travel to distant, strange places. They must also defeat a powerful enemy. Both myths and science fiction use such plots.

Reading

Main idea: Science fiction and myths have many things in common.
Key points:
- _____ in science fiction are similar to the ones in myths.
- _____ of science fiction and myths are similar.

Lecture

Main idea: *Star Wars* is similar in many ways to ancient myths.
Key points:
- The hero of *Star Wars* is very _____
  - He can use _____
  - He also finds out he is _____
- _____ is also similar to myths.
  - The hero's journey begins when _____
  - The hero's _____

C. Read the prompt.

Summarize the main points made in the lecture and explain how they support the main points in the reading passage.

D. Fill in the blanks of the sample response using phrases from the box. Use your notes to help you.

The reading says that _____ are often very similar. The author supports this with two points. First, the characters in science fiction and myths can be _____. In addition, _____ that the plots of science fiction and myths are often similar.

The lecture supports the reading using the example of *Star Wars*. The speaker first discusses the characters in *Star Wars* using _____ as an example. The speaker says that Luke can use a magical power like many heroes in myths. In addition, he finds out in the story that he is royalty, which often happens to the heroes in myths. Second, the author says that *Star Wars* has a plot similar to myths. First, _____ begins when his home is destroyed. In addition, the _____ of the hero are similar to other heroes in myths.

the author states	science fiction and myths
motives	the hero, Luke,
the hero's journey	very similar

E. Fill in the blanks with the correct words.

legend	plot	evident	tragedy	motive

1. Many story writers prefer to first write the _____, while some prefer to start with the characters.
2. It is much easier to understand people when you know the _____ that causes them to act a certain way.
3. One Greek _____ involves a mythical hero named Hercules.
4. After the fire, the family made sure their house was protected against fire in order to prevent a similar _____.
5. His interest in the school project was _____ from his hard, enthusiastic work.

Test

Step 1

Read the passage. Then listen to the lecture. Take notes in the boxes below. `Track 31`

Science Fiction

People write science fiction for many reasons. Some like to imagine a future world. Others want to use a future world to comment on the current world. Science fiction is often a way for authors to offer their views of the world. Authors can often do this in two ways.

The first is to offer comments on the current world by imagining the world in the future. Many authors think the world will look very different in the future. However, many of the same problems may still exist. Some authors use science fiction to talk about the problems that the world has.

The second way authors use this is to talk about how the world will be in the future. Some authors think we might not solve some problems in the future. Thus, authors use future worlds to show what life will be like if we don't solve these problems.

Reading

Main idea: Some writers use science fiction to comment on the world.
Key points:
- Some authors comment on the world by _____
- Authors also write science fiction to _____

_____

Lecture

Main idea: *The War of the Worlds* was a story that was meant to comment on the world.
Key points:
- It commented on _____
  - In the story, aliens _____
  - Wells was _____
- He was also _____
  - Wells believed that _____
  - He described how _____

Step 2

Read and listen to the prompt. `Track 32`

Summarize the main points made in the lecture and explain how they support the main points in the reading passage.

Step 3

Complete the outline using your notes from Step 1.

Topic: Science fiction can be a way for authors to offer social commentary.

A. The reading says that authors _____

    1. First, some authors _____

    2. Also, authors write _____

    _____

B. The lecture supports the reading by _____

    _____

    1. It commented on _____

      • In the story, _____

      • With this, Wells was _____

    2. He was also _____

      • Wells believed that _____

      • He described how _____

Conclusion: Wells's story supports the reading because _____

_____.

Step 4

Complete the response using your outline from Step 3.

The reading and the lecture say that _____

_____.

The reading says _____.

First, some authors _____.

Also, _____

_____.

The lecture _____

_____.

It commented on _____.

In the story, _____.

With this, _____.

He was also _____.

Wells believed that _____.

He described how _____.

In conclusion, Wells's story _____

_____.

Check-up

Fill in the blanks with the correct words.

lungs	second-hand smoke	quest	cancer
myth	non-smokers	hero	royalty

1. The king, queen, and their relatives are all considered _____.

2. Smoking can damage the _____, making it difficult to breathe.

3. Many historians who study ancient cultures must decide if a story is history or just a _____.

4. _____ is a serious disease with no known cure.

5. There is evidence to suggest that breathing _____ is just as dangerous as smoking.

6. A common _____ for a story's main character is to leave on a journey in search of a magical item.

7. Many _____ want smoking banned in public places.

8. The _____ of many stories must battle with an enemy before the story is complete.

[8] Independent

Getting Ready to Write

A. Learn the words.

Key Vocabulary

suburb	a community around a city
commute	the trip from home to a workplace
traffic	the vehicles moving on a road
distance	the amount of space between two places

TOEFL® Vocabulary

downtown	the center or main part of a city or town
exhausted	feeling very tired
maximize	to increase something as much as possible
fatigue	the feeling of being tired
to sum up	to review the main points; in conclusion

B. Read the prompt. Then answer the questions.

Describe the area where you live.

1. What kind of community do you live in?

My community is _____.

2. Is your school close to where you live?

My school is _____.

3. How long does it take you to get from your home to your school?

It takes _____.

4. What do you like about where you live?

I like _____.

Practice

A. Read the question.

Do you agree or disagree with the following statement?

It is better to live close to work.

Use specific reasons and examples to support your answer.

B. Read the sample response. Then answer the question.

I think it is better to live close to where you work. I feel this way for two reasons. The first reason is that living close to work saves time and money. For example, I live in the suburbs but have a job downtown. It takes me two hours to travel a distance of ten miles because the traffic has been bad lately. If I worked closer to my home, I could spend less time in my car and I could save a lot of money, too. Another benefit of living close to work is that you are less tired at the end of the day. All the time I spend driving to and from work makes me feel exhausted. When I lived and worked near my old job, I had more free time. It was easier to just come home at the end of the day and relax or meet some friends for a game of tennis. In fact, living close to work allowed me to maximize my free time and feel less fatigue. It was much better than the situation I have now. For these reasons, I think it is better to live close to where you work.

Which side of the statement does the response take?
(A) Agree   (B) Disagree

C. Complete the outline for the response.

Topic: It is better to live _____ where you work.
A. Living close to work saves _____
   1. If you live close to work, you can get there _____
   2. If you live close to your job, _____
B. Another benefit of living close to work is _____
   1. Driving can make you _____
   2. If you live close to work, you'll _____
Conclusion: I think it is better to _____ to where you work.

D. Underline the transitional words or phrases in the sample response.

E. Read the sample response. Then answer the question.

I think that it isn't good to live close to where you work. There are two reasons why I feel this way. First, I need to have distance between my work life and my personal life. I like to keep them separate, and a long commute helps me to do that. For instance, I had a job this summer in another town. When I drove to work, I liked to use that time to prepare for my day. Similarly, I usually felt exhausted at the end of the day, but when I drove home, I could listen to music and forget about my fatigue. Not living close to work has helped me maximize the separation between my work life and my personal life. Second, I want a career in finance, which means I will work for a company located downtown. However, I don't want to live downtown since I prefer the suburbs. Therefore, I would rather live some distance away from where I work. To sum up, I think that it's actually better not to live close to where you work.

Which side of the statement does the response take?

(A) Agree   (B) Disagree

Outline

F. Complete the outline for the response.

Topic: It _____ to live close to where you work.

A. I need to have distance between _____
   1. I like to keep them separate, and _____ helps me do that.
   2. It also helps me maximize the separation between _____
   _____

B. I want a career in finance, which means I will work for _____
   1. I don't want to live downtown since _____
   2. I would rather live some distance _____
Conclusion: I think that it's actually better _____ close to where you work.

G. Underline the transitional words or phrases in the sample response.

TOEFL® Vocabulary Practice

H. Fill in the blanks with the correct words.

| downtown | exhausted | fatigue | maximize | to sum up |

1. By planning carefully, you can _____ your studying time.

2. After the race, George was overcome with _____ and nearly passed out.

3. _____, our plan is to build a park that everyone can enjoy.

4. If you want to see skyscrapers, you will have to go _____.

5. When I get home from work, I am usually too _____ to cook dinner.

Test

Step 1

Read the question.

Do you agree or disagree with the following statement?

It is better to live close to work.

Use specific reasons and examples to support your answer

Step 2

State your opinion.

I _____ with the statement.

Step 3

Write an outline for your essay that will support your decision.

Topic: _____.
A. _____
    1. _____
    2. _____
B. _____
    1. _____
    2. _____
Conclusion: _____.

Step 4

Complete the response using your own outline from above.

I think that _____.
First, _____
_____.
For instance, _____
_____.
In addition, _____
_____.
Second, _____.
For example, _____
_____.
Also, _____
_____.
To sum up, _____.

Getting Ready to Write

A. Learn the words.

Key Vocabulary

ethanol	a chemical that is made from plants and can be used as fuel
fossil fuel	a fuel such as gasoline or coal
refine	to remove things from a substance to make it better
refinement	the process of removing something from a substance

TOEFL® Vocabulary

substitute	something that is used when a similar thing can't be used
negate	to make something not have an effect
sustainable	able to be continued for a long time
label	to use a word or phrase to describe something
notwithstanding	despite

Reading Passage

B. Read the first part of a passage. Then answer the questions.

> **Ethanol**
>
> Some people have said that ethanol can be a substitute for fossil fuels. Ethanol comes mostly from corn. The sugar from corn is used to make ethanol. There are many problems with ethanol, however. Two of these problems negate its few benefits.

1. What is the main idea of the passage?

(A) The different ways to make ethanol fuel

(B) The problems of using ethanol as fuel

2. What do you think the rest of the passage will talk about? Write two or three ideas below.

_____

_____

Practice

A. Listen to the first part of a lecture. Then answer the question. `Track 33`

What is the main idea of the lecture?

(A) A theory about ethanol use in twenty years

(B) Reasons why arguments against ethanol are incorrect

B. Read the full passage. Then listen to the full lecture. Take notes in the boxes below. `Track 34`

Ethanol

Some people have said that ethanol can be a substitute for fossil fuels. Ethanol comes mostly from corn. The sugar from corn is used to make ethanol. There are many problems with ethanol, however. Two of these problems negate its few benefits.

First, it takes more energy to make ethanol than it can produce. The corn must first be grown. This requires some energy. Before it can be used as fuel, ethanol must be refined. The refinement process needs fuel. The process doesn't make enough fuel to match how much fuel was used. It only makes the energy problem worse.

In addition, a lot of land is needed to grow corn. Some people say ethanol is good because it is sustainable. There isn't enough land to grow all the corn that we would need, though. Ethanol could only replace a small part of our fuel. People would still have to use gasoline.

Reading

Main idea: The problems with ethanol negate its benefits.
Key points:
- It takes more _____ to make ethanol than _____
- Too much _____ is needed to grow the corn needed for ethanol.

Lecture

Main idea: The points against ethanol are not correct.
Key points:
- Some people say making ethanol uses _____
  - It is easier to _____
  - Ethanol now creates _____
- Others say we would need _____
  - Scientists have come up with _____
  - In the future, less _____

C. Read the prompt.

Summarize the main points made in the lecture and explain how they differ from the main points in the reading passage.

D. Fill in the blanks of the sample response using phrases from the box. Use your notes to help you.

The reading says that there are many problems with using ethanol as fuel, and these problems negate _____. The author uses two points to support this. First, ethanol _____ as much energy as is needed to make it. In addition, too much land is needed to grow the corn needed for ethanol.

_____ with the points made in the reading. The speaker mentions that some people think ethanol does not make enough energy. However, it is easier _____ ethanol today. Ethanol now creates more energy than is needed to make it. In addition, the speaker says that _____ that too much land is needed to make ethanol. However, scientists have come up with new ways to make ethanol. In the future, less corn _____ to make the same amount of ethanol.

will be needed	does not produce
some people think	to make
its benefits	The lecture disagrees

E. Fill in the blanks with the correct words.

substitute   negate   sustainable   label   notwithstanding

1. Some people _____ global warming the world's biggest problem.

2. If a school teacher is sick for a day, the school must ask a _____ to teach the class.

3. _____ the sometimes bitter taste, many people around the world drink coffee each day.

4. The many benefits of daily exercise _____ the argument that there isn't enough time in a day to exercise.

5. Hydrogen power is one of the many possibilities in the search for a _____ energy source.

Test

Step 1

Read the passage. Then listen to the lecture. Take notes in the boxes below. **Track 35**

New Sources of Energy

The world is looking for new sources of energy. Many have said we should use wind power. In fact, some countries have already begun to use wind power. In Denmark, 20% of the country's electricity comes from the wind. Wind power should be used as an energy source for two reasons.

First, wind power does not pollute the environment. Fossil fuels send harmful gases into the atmosphere. Wind farms, however, do not. Making wind power does not produce any harmful pollution. In other words, it is a clean energy source.

Second, wind power is sustainable. Unlike fossil fuels, wind power will never run out. As there will always be wind, there will always be wind power. The only issue is finding ways to change the wind into power. Wind power is being used more often. As long as this trend goes on, wind power can replace fossil fuels.

Reading

Main idea: Wind power should be used as a replacement for fossil fuels.
Key points:
- Wind power does not _____
- Wind power is _____

Lecture

Main idea: There are two major problems with wind power.
Key points:
- Wind power does _____
  - Fossil fuels _____
  - Wind power _____
- Wind power is not _____
  - Some places do not have _____
  - Without wind, _____

Step 2

Read and listen to the prompt. **Track 36**

Summarize the main points made in the lecture and explain how they differ from the main points in the reading passage.

Step 3

Complete the outline using your notes from Step 1.

Topic: Whether wind power should be used as a replacement for fossil fuels.

A. The reading says that wind power _____

    1. Wind power does not _____

    2. Wind power is _____

B. The lecture says that there are _____

    1. Wind power does _____

      • Fossil fuels _____

      • Wind power _____

    2. Wind power is not _____

      • Some places _____

      • Without wind, _____

Conclusion: Wind power is _____.

Step 4

Complete the response using your outline from Step 3.

The reading and the lecture discuss _____
_____.

The reading says _____
_____.

To begin, wind power does not _____.

Additionally, wind power is _____.

    The lecture _____.

First, wind power does _____.

Fossil fuels _____.

Wind power _____.

Second, the speaker says that wind power is not _____.

Some places _____.

Without wind, _____.

    In conclusion, the lecture says that _____.

Check-up

Fill in the blanks with the correct words.

suburbs	commute	traffic	distance
ethanol	fossil fuel	refine	refinement

1. Before oil can be used as a fuel, it must go through a process of _____.
2. The largest source of _____ in the United States is corn.
3. Many people prefer to work in the city but live in the _____.
4. In order to _____ oil, certain chemicals must be added to it.
5. A long _____ to work can leave you feeling tired at the end of the day.
6. The more _____ there is on the road, the more pollution there will be.
7. Coal is a(n) _____ that was used even in the Middle Ages.
8. The _____ from the Earth to the Sun is millions of kilometers.

[9] Independent

Getting Ready to Write

A. Learn the words.

editor	the person who decides what to include in a newspaper or magazine
report	a written description of something
democratic	related to a system that allows everyone to participate
accept	to take something offered to you

reliable	able to be trusted; dependable
document	to write or film something in order to record it for future use
assert	to state firmly that something is true
professional	someone who has specialized skills or training
journalism	the job of writing news reports for newspapers, TV, or radio

B. Read the prompt. Then answer the questions.

Describe how you use the Internet.

1. What do you use the Internet for?
   I use the Internet _____.

2. What do your friends use the Internet for?
   They use the Internet _____.

3. Have you ever used the Internet to do homework?
   I have _____.

4. Why don't some people like the Internet?
   They don't like the Internet because _____.

Practice

A. Read the question.

Do you agree or disagree with the following statement?

The Internet does not give reliable information.

Use specific reasons and examples to support your answer.

B. Read the sample response. Then answer the question.

I think that the Internet does not give reliable information. There are two reasons why I think this way. One is that anyone can write whatever they want and put it on the Internet. The other is that on the Internet, people don't document where their information comes from. First, anyone can assert that something is correct or true on the Internet. However, sometimes they are wrong, or they are lying. When you read a newspaper or book, you can trust the information. Editors have made sure that it is correct and true. That is not the case with the Internet. Second, professional writers must document where they get their information from. However, on the Internet, many people don't know the source of the reports they read. This is unlike journalism. In journalism, you must tell where you get your information. You do this to make sure it is reliable. Then readers can trust you. To sum up, the Internet is not a good source of reliable information.

Which side of the statement does the response take?
(A) Agree   (B) Disagree

C. Complete the outline for the response.

Topic: The Internet _____ reliable information.
  A. Anyone can write whatever they want and _____
      1. When you read a newspaper or book, _____
      2. That is not the case _____
  B. On the Internet, people don't document where _____
      1. On the Internet, many people don't know _____
      2. In journalism, you must tell where you get your information from so that it is
              _____ and readers _____
Conclusion: The Internet is _____ source of reliable information.

D. Underline the transitional words or phrases in the sample response.

E. Read the sample response. Then answer the question.

I think the Internet gives reliable information. I think this for two reasons. First, the Internet is democratic. It allows anyone with a computer to share information. This is a good thing because it makes it easier for people to talk with each other. If someone asserts something that is not true, someone else will correct them. They don't have to accept it. With the Internet, you don't need a degree in journalism to publish information. Second, you can get excellent information about products on the Internet. This can help you make good decisions when you want to buy something. For example, I needed a new bike. I didn't want to go to the bike shop. The people there are not friendly. Instead, I got on the Internet. I read what other people said about different brands of bikes. Some of the people were professionals. That made it easier for me to make a decision. I got the bike I wanted. In summary, you can find lots of reliable information on the Internet.

Which side of the statement does the response take?

(A) Agree   (B) Disagree

F. Complete the outline for the response.

Topic: I think the Internet _____ reliable information.
A. The Internet is democratic because it allows anyone with a computer _____
   _____
   1. This is a good thing because it makes it easier for people to _____
   2. If someone says something that is not true, _____
B. You can get excellent information about _____
   1. This can help you make good decisions when _____
   2. When I needed a new bike, I used the Internet to _____
Conclusion: You _____ reliable information on the Internet.

G. Underline the transitional words or phrases in the sample response.

H. Fill in the blanks with the correct words.

assert   document   journalism   profession   reliable

1. The teacher asked the students to _____ every step of their science projects.
2. The most _____ people are the ones the company cannot do without.
3. If you do not _____ the truth, then many people will never know it.
4. You often must study for many years before you can join a(n) _____.
5. People say that I should study _____ and become a reporter.

Test

Step 1

Read the question.

Do you agree or disagree with the following statement?

The Internet does not give reliable information.

Use specific reasons and examples to support your answer.

Step 2

State your opinion.

I _____ with the statement.

Step 3

Write an outline for your essay that will support your opinion.

Topic: The Internet _____ reliable information.

A. _____

   1. _____

   2. _____

B. _____

   1. _____

   2. _____

Conclusion: The Internet is _____ of reliable information.

Step 4

Complete the response using your outline from above.

    I think that _____.

I think this for two reasons. First, _____.

For example, _____

_____.

In addition, _____

_____.

Second, _____.

This means _____

_____.

However, _____.

In summary, _____.

Getting Ready to Write

A. Learn the words.

Key Vocabulary

chronic	happening often and in a regular way
hormone	a natural chemical produced by the human body
diabetes	a disease that makes the body unable to store sugars correctly
insulin	a substance in the body that controls how much sugar is in the blood

TOEFL® Vocabulary

psychological	involving how the mind works
mental	having to do with the mind
regulate	to control something in order to make it work correctly
logic	the ability to connect ideas
acquisition	the process of learning new things

Reading Passage

B. Read the first part of a passage. Then answer the questions.

Sleep

Doctors recommend at least eight hours of sleep each night. What happens when you get fewer than eight hours? Scientists say that chronic sleep loss can have many psychological effects. It can also change the way the body works.

1. What is the main idea of the passage?

    (A) The effects of not getting enough sleep

    (B) What happens to the brain during sleep

2. What do you think the rest of the passage will talk about? Write two or three ideas below.

    _____

    _____

Practice

A. Listen to the first part of a lecture. Then answer the question. Track 37

What is the main idea of the lecture?

(A) The results of a study on sleep loss

(B) Refuting the idea that sleep loss affects the mind

B. Read the full passage. Then listen to the full lecture. Take notes in the boxes below. Track 38

Sleep

Doctors recommend at least eight hours of sleep each night. What happens when you get fewer than eight hours? Scientists say that chronic sleep loss can have many psychological effects. It can also change the way the body works.

To begin, sleep loss can change mental function. People are most alert when they get over eight hours of sleep. Getting fewer than eight hours of sleep can change how the brain works. The brain struggles to do easy tasks. This places stress on the brain. Chronic sleep loss, then, can harm the brain.

Secondly, sleep loss also changes how the body works. With over eight hours of sleep, the body produces normal levels of hormones. This can affect people in many ways. In the short-term, it can simply change how the body regulates itself. Over time, however, sleep loss can lead to certain diseases.

Reading

Main idea: Sleep loss can have many negative effects on the mind.
Key points:
- Sleep loss can change the way _____
- Sleep loss also changes how _____

Lecture

Main idea: A study on sleep loss found two conclusions.
Key points:
- People didn't seem _____
  - Their ability to use _____ wasn't very good.
  - Even the _____ was affected.
- Sleep loss also affects the way _____ works.
  - It affects how the body produces _____
  - The body doesn't _____ when someone doesn't get enough sleep.

C. Read the prompt.

Summarize the main points made in the lecture and explain how they support the main points in the reading passage.

D. Fill in the blanks of the sample response using phrases from the box. Use your notes to help you.

The reading says that _____ can have many effects on the mind and body. _____ two points to support this. To begin, the author says that sleep loss can affect how the mind works. In addition, it can make the body work incorrectly.

The lecture _____ with a study. The speaker begins by describing the study. The study found two conclusions. First, the study found that people didn't seem _____ when they didn't get enough sleep. Their ability to use logic to solve problems wasn't very good. In addition, the way they learned was also affected. Second, the speaker says that sleep loss affects the way the body works. It changes the way the body _____. The body is unable to _____ correctly when a person doesn't get enough sleep.

sleep loss	produces insulin
as alert or smart	supports the reading
make it	The author offers

E. Fill in the blanks with the correct words.

psychological   mentally   regulate   logic   acquisition

1. The body is naturally able to _____ a person's breathing when he or she is asleep.
2. Some scientists worry about the _____ effects of television violence.
3. A good night's sleep can make a person more _____ aware throughout the day.
4. The process of language _____ begins very early in a child's life.
5. Many examinations are designed to test a student's _____.

Test

Step 1

> ### Sleep Loss
>
> Scientists agree that sleep loss is bad for the brain. Many people, though, don't know what happens in the brain when you don't get enough sleep. The brain's ability to learn new things suffers. Thus, lack of sleep can make it harder to learn simple things. There are two ways that this happens.
>
> First, sleep loss can make it harder to remember directions. Scientists call this spatial learning, or the ability to learn how to get to certain places. Sleep loss makes it harder to remember how to get to a new place. Thus, even moving around in the world is hard if you don't get enough sleep.
>
> In addition, sleep loss makes the brain unable to rest. Even the brain needs to rest and recover, and when the brain can't rest, it isn't able to learn new things effectively. Therefore, sleep loss keeps the brain from learning as well as it should.

Reading

Main idea: Lack of sleep can make it difficult for the brain to learn new things.
Key points:
- Sleep loss can make it harder to _____
- Sleep loss makes the brain unable to _____

Lecture

Main idea: A study of sleep loss in rats found two things.
Key points:
- Rats can't _____ when they don't get enough sleep.
  - Rested rats could easily remember _____
  - Rats that didn't sleep couldn't remember _____
- Sleep loss keeps the brain from _____
  - When the rats didn't sleep, a part of the brain _____
  - It couldn't make _____ in that area.

Step 2

Summarize the main points made in the lecture and explain how they support the main points in the reading passage.

Step 3

Complete the outline using your notes from Step 1.

Topic: The effects of lack of sleep on the brain.

A. The reading says that lack of sleep can make it difficult for the brain _____

_____

    1. Sleep loss can make it harder to _____

    2. Sleep loss makes the brain unable to _____

B. The lecture describes a _____

    1. Rats can't _____

       • Rested rats could easily _____

       • Rats that didn't sleep _____

    2. Sleep loss keeps the brain from _____

       • When the rats didn't sleep, _____

       • It couldn't make _____

Conclusion: Sleep loss keeps the brain from _____.

Step 4

Complete the response using your outline from Step 3.

    The reading and the lecture discuss _____.

The reading says that lack of sleep _____.

First, sleep loss can make it _____.

Also, sleep loss makes the brain _____.

    The lecture describes a _____.

First, the speaker says that rats can't _____

_____.

Rested rats could easily _____.

Rats that didn't sleep _____.

Second, the speaker says sleep loss keeps the brain from _____.

When the rats didn't sleep, _____.

It couldn't make _____.

    In conclusion, the lecture supports the reading by _____

_____.

Check-up

Fill in the blanks with the correct words.

editor	democratic	reports	accept
chronic	hormone	diabetes	insulin

1. A(n) _____ is a chemical that carries messages in the body.

2. When a person has _____, his or her body does not control sugars properly.

3. Children should not _____ gifts from strangers.

4. The US has a(n) _____ system of government.

5. The _____ of a newspaper decides which stories will be printed.

6. Many people who look at computer screens all day can have _____ headaches.

7. If a person's body does not have enough _____, doctors can provide a shot to help.

8. Scientists must write up _____ describing their experiments.

[10] Independent

Getting Ready to Write

A. Learn the words.

stingy	unwilling to share or give to others
philanthropy	the practice of giving away a lot of money
generous	willing to share or give to others
market economy	an economic system not controlled by government

proper	correct
compensation	money or gifts given to a person in exchange for their work
wealth	the amount of money a person owns
role	the function of something in an activity
proportion	a number or amount in relation to a whole

B. Read the prompt. Then answer the questions.

Describe an experience when someone gave you money.

1. What was the experience?
   The experience was _____.

2. Who did you receive the money from?
   I received the money from _____.

3. Why did they give you money?
   They gave me money _____.

4. What did you do with the money?
   I _____.

Practice

A. Read the question.

Do you agree or disagree with the following statement?

> Rich people should give money to poor people.

Use specific reasons and examples to support your answer.

B. Read the sample response. Then answer the question.

I think that rich people should not give money to the poor. There are two reasons I feel this way. First, rich people work hard and deserve to keep all the money they earn. It is not proper to take their money. We live in a market economy in which anyone can become rich. Some people work harder than other people do. They study for many years in college, or they take risks in business. Therefore, those people should get more compensation for their efforts. Moreover, when they work hard, they will increase their wealth, and they deserve to keep it. Second, giving money to poor people will make them lazy. If poor people want more money, they will have to work for it. That is how a market economy works. You get what you deserve, and you choose your role in society. If you want to be rich, you will be rich. In conclusion, I think that rich people should not give money to poor people, as it is not a good idea.

Which side of the statement does the response take?
(A) Agree   (B) Disagree

C. Complete the outline for the response.

Topic: Rich people _____ give money to the poor.
   A. Rich people work hard and deserve to _____
       1. It is not proper _____
       2. Some people work _____
   B. Giving money to poor people will _____
       1. If poor people want more money, they _____
       2. That is how a market economy _____
Conclusion: Rich people _____ give money to poor people.

D. Underline the transitional words or phrases in the sample response.

E. Read the sample response. Then answer the question.

    I think that rich people should give money to the poor. I think there are two reasons they should do this. First, most rich people have more money than they need. They use a very small proportion of their wealth. That means they have a lot of extra money. For this reason, they should give some of their money away to help people who have less. They shouldn't be stingy. Many people do not have their basic needs met, such as housing, food, or clothes. Rich people should help them. Secondly, rich people have a responsibility to the society that gave them their riches. Not everyone can become rich. When you work hard, sometimes you will still be poor. Rich people, therefore, should use their money to help other people enjoy things. They should build museums, libraries, and other places that are free to the public. Society makes some people rich. It is therefore their proper role to give back to society through philanthropy. When I am rich, I will be generous with my money. For the above reasons, I think the rich should give money to the poor.

Which side of the statement does the response take?

(A) Agree   (B) Disagree

Outline

F. Complete the outline for the response.

Topic: Rich people _____ give money to the poor.
  A. Most rich people have more _____
      1. They should give some of their money away to _____
      2. Many people do not have their basic needs met, such as _____
      _____

  B. Rich people have a responsibility to _____
      1. Not everyone can _____
      2. Rich people, therefore, should use their money to _____
Conclusion: I think the rich _____ give money to the poor.

G. Underline the transitional words or phrases in the sample response.

TOEFL® Vocabulary Practice

H. Fill in the blanks with the correct words.

compensation	proper	proportion	role	wealth

1. Someday, I hope to have enough _____ to build a museum for my city.
2. The _____ of people who are rich is small compared to everyone in the country.
3. I want to work for a company that gives its employees excellent _____.
4. Sara has been practicing singing so she can get the lead _____ in the school play.
5. When you receive a gift, the _____ thing to do is to say "thank you."

Test

Step 1

Read the question.

Do you agree or disagree with the following statement?

Rich people should give money to poor people.

Use specific reasons and examples to support your answer.

Step 2

State your opinion.

I _____ with the statement.

Step 3

Write an outline for your essay that will support your opinion.

Topic: Rich people _____ give money to the poor.

A. _____

    1. _____

    2. _____

B. _____

    1. _____

    2. _____

Conclusion: I think that rich people _____.

Step 4

Complete the response using your outline from above.

I think that _____.

I think this for two reasons. First, _____

_____.

I think _____.

Also, _____.

Secondly, _____.

This means that _____.

In addition, _____

_____.

It is for these reasons that _____.

Integrated - Technology

Getting Ready to Write

A. Learn the words.

Key Vocabulary

transistor	a part that controls the electricity inside electronic equipment
expected	believed to happen soon or at a certain future time
trend	the general movement of events in a likely way
someday	at some uncertain time in the future

TOEFL® Vocabulary

capacity	the amount of something that a thing can have inside of it
credible	able to be believed
mere	small or unimportant
guideline	a statement that says how someone should do something in the future
solely	only for the reason stated

Reading Passage

B. Read the first part of a passage. Then answer the questions.

Technology

It seems that technology moves too fast. Just when you think you have the latest device, a new one comes out. The growth of computer power is described by Moore's Law. This law says that the capacity of transistors on a chip will double each year. In simple terms, this means that computers get faster at a steady rate. People support this theory with two facts.

1. What is the main idea of the passage?

   (A) How transistors work in computers

   (B) Reasons why Moore's Law is true

2. What do you think the rest of the passage will talk about? Write two or three ideas below.

   _____

   _____

Practice

A. Listen to the first part of a lecture. Then answer the question. `Track 41`

What is the main idea of the lecture?

(A) How we can follow Moore's Law

(B) Why Moore's Law is not true

Note-taking

B. Read the full passage. Then listen to the full lecture. Take notes in the boxes below. `Track 42`

Technology

It seems that technology moves too fast. Just when you think you have the latest device, a new one comes out. The growth of computer power is described by Moore's Law. This law says that the capacity of transistors on a chip will double each year. In simple terms, this means that computers get faster at a steady rate. People support this theory with two facts.

First, Moore's Law has been true for many years. Chips are getting faster each year. Even other things are affected. Cameras also improve in an expected way each year.

Second, people believe that Moore's Law will be true in the future too. Since it has been true for so long, people see no reason for it to change now. In addition, people are coming up with new ways to make chips. This will help computer makers follow the trend.

Reading

Main idea: The theory of Moore's Law can be supported with two facts.
Key points:
- Moore's Law has been _____
- Moore's Law will be true _____

Lecture

Main idea: Moore's Law will not be true at some point in the future.
Key points:
- Moore's Law is only true because people _____
  - Computer makers try to _____
  - It wouldn't be true if _____
- It has been true in the past, but it can't _____
  - Someday, computer makers won't be able to _____
  - When this happens, Moore's Law _____

C. Read the prompt.

Summarize the main points made in the lecture and explain how they differ from the main points in the reading passage.

D. Fill in the blanks of the sample response using phrases from the box. Use your notes to help you.

The reading describes Moore's Law and gives reasons why it is true. _____ that it can be supported with two facts. First, _____ has been true in the past. In addition, Moore's Law will continue for many years in the future.

The lecture _____ the reading. The speaker gives two reasons to support the idea that Moore's Law is not a real law. First, Moore's Law is only true because people _____. Computer makers try to follow Moore's Law. If they didn't do this, the law would not be true. In addition, it has been true _____, but it can't go on forever. Someday, computer makers won't be able to fit _____ on a chip. When this happens, Moore's Law will no longer be true.

The author says	Moore's Law
more transistors	want it to be true
in the past	disagrees with

E. Fill in the blanks with the correct words.

capacity   credible   mere   solely   guidelines

1. The _____ of computer hard drives is now often over 100 gigabytes.

2. While some see credit card debt as a _____ annoyance, it can be a very serious problem.

3. Only the results of _____ polls and surveys are likely to be trusted by the public.

4. Lawyers must follow a set of _____ in order to practice law in a state.

5. A science teacher usually teaches classes _____ about the various sciences.

Test

Step 1

Read the passage. Then listen to the lecture. Take notes in the boxes below. Track 43

> ### Artificial Intelligence
>
> Some people think we will one day have artificial intelligence, or AI. An AI is a computer that can think. For a computer to be intelligent, it has to learn and reason without the help of people. So far, this has not happened. However, many people think that it will someday in the future. There are two reasons to think that we will one day have AI.
>
> First, some computers can now learn. In the past, computers had to be programmed to do things. Now, computers can learn to do new things. They learn these new things with only some programming. In the future, they may be able to learn without any programming at all.
>
> In addition, some computers know how to reason. Computers can win chess matches against real people. They can solve chess problems even when they aren't told how to solve them. One computer, called Deep Blue, beat a famous chess player in 1997. Soon, computers will be able to do even more impressive tasks.

Reading

Main idea: We will someday have artificially intelligent computers.
Key points:
- Computers can now _____
- Some computers now know how to _____

Lecture

Main idea: Computers will never be able to think.
Key points:
- Computers are not able to _____
  - The only reason computers can learn is because _____
  - It isn't learning; it is just _____
- Computers will never be able to _____
  - Humans have _____ that machines will never have.
  - Machines can only solve problems that _____

Step 2

Read and listen to the prompt. Track 44

Summarize the main points made in the lecture and explain how they differ from the main points in the reading passage.

Step 3

Complete the outline using your notes from Step 1.

Topic: Whether computers will ever be able to think.

A. We will someday have _____

    1. Computers can now _____

    2. Some computers now know _____

B. The lecture says computers _____

    1. Computers are not able to _____

       • The only reason computers can learn is _____

       • It isn't learning; it is _____

    2. Computers will never be able to _____

       • Humans have _____

       • Machines can only solve problems that _____

Conclusion: Therefore, machines _____.

Step 4

Complete the sample response using your outline from Step 3.

    The reading and the lecture discuss _____.

The reading says _____.

Computers can now _____.

Also, some computers now know _____.

    The lecture says computers _____.

First, computers are not able to _____. The only reason computers

can learn is _____.

It isn't learning; it is _____.

Second, computers will never be able to _____.

Humans have _____.

Machines can only solve problems that _____.

    In conclusion, the lecture disagrees with the reading because it says _____

_____.

Check-up

Fill in the blanks with the correct words.

stingy	philanthropy	generous	market economy
trend	transistors	expected	someday

1. _____, we may have automobiles that can drive themselves to destinations.

2. _____ people don't like to share things.

3. The progress of computers has so far followed a(n) _____ process of development.

4. Bill Gates is becoming famous for his _____ as well as his business.

5. Some computer chips can contain over one billion _____.

6. Communist countries do not believe in a(n) _____.

7. The _____ of fast computers is likely to continue for many years.

8. _____ people often have many friends.

[11] Independent

Getting Ready to Write

A. Learn the words.

Key Vocabulary

value	what something is worth
college	a school that students can go to after high school
plenty	a lot of
point	reason

TOEFL® Vocabulary

former	coming before; previous
circumstance	the condition that affects a situation
contribution	something you give to help something be successful
generation	all the people of about the same age
framework	the structure or organization of something

B. Read the prompt. Then answer the questions.

Describe a historical figure from your country.

1. Who is this person?
   This person is _____.

2. What did this person do?
   This person was _____.

3. Why do students learn about this person?
   They learn about _____ because _____.

4. If you could meet this person, what would you ask him/her?
   I would ask _____.

Practice

A. Read the question.

Do you agree or disagree with the following statement?

Learning about the past has no value for those living today.

Use specific reasons and examples to support your answer.

B. Read the sample response. Then answer the question.

I think that learning about the past has no value for those living today. I feel this way for two reasons. First, the world today is very different than it was in the past. Thus, learning about how people lived in the past is useless. Today, circumstances are so different from those in the past. Getting food is one example. We don't need to know how people used to grow food. Nobody lives that way anymore; therefore, knowing the past can't make any contribution to our lives today. Secondly, learning about the past wastes our time. That time could be better spent learning other subjects. We can then prepare for the future. For example, if I didn't have to take history classes in high school, I could have taken more computer classes. This would help me prepare for college. It would also help me get a better job in the future. I feel like history class is a waste of time. In conclusion, I don't think there is any point to learning about the past.

Which side of the statement did the response take?
(A) Agree   (B) Disagree

C. Complete the outline for the response.

Topic: Learning about the past has _____ for those living today.
A. The world today is _____ than it was in the past.
   1. Learning about how people lived _____
   2. Today, circumstances are so _____
B. Learning about the past _____
   1. Learning about other subjects would help me _____
   2. Taking a computer class would also help me _____
Conclusion: I don't think there is any point to _____.

D. Underline the transitional words or phrases in the sample response.

E. Read the sample response. Then answer the question.

I think that learning about the past has a lot of value for those living today. There are two reasons. One reason is that our traditions remind us of who we are. They contain the wisdom of former generations. Therefore, they give us a framework for how to live our lives. If we throw away our traditions, we will forget where we come from. We will become lost. Second, learning about the past can help us make decisions. It can also help us avoid making the same mistakes again. Since the beginning of time, people have tried to do plenty of things. Sometimes, they failed. For example, people built cities near volcanoes. The cities were destroyed. We can study these mistakes. This can help us avoid them. This is one of the most important contributions history can make to our lives today. For these reasons, I think it is very valuable for people today to learn about the past.

Which side of the statement does the response take?
(A) Agree   (B) Disagree

Outline

F. Complete the outline for the response.

Topic: Learning about the past has _____ for those living today.
A. Our traditions remind us _____
   1. They contain the wisdom of former generations; therefore, _____
   _____
   2. If we throw away our traditions, _____
B. Learning about the past can help us _____
   1. It can also help us avoid _____
   2. We can study _____
Conclusion: I think it is _____ for people today to learn about the past.

G. Underline the transitional words or phrases in the sample response.

TOEFL® Vocabulary Practice

H. Fill in the blanks with the correct words.

circumstance	contribution	former	generation	framework

1. Once you prepare the _____, you can then fill in the details.
2. Many people of the older _____ are not comfortable using computers.
3. Bill Clinton is a _____ president of the US.
4. Can you think of a _____ in which it is OK to lie?
5. Taking the photographs was my _____ to the project.

Test

Step 1

Read the question.

Do you agree or disagree with the following statement?

Learning about the past has no value for those living today.

Use specific reasons and examples to support your answer.

Step 2

State your opinion.

I _____ with the statement.

Step 3

Write an outline for your essay that will support your opinion.

Topic: Learning about the past _____ value for those living today.

A. _____

    1. _____

    2. _____

B. _____

    1. _____

    2. _____

Conclusion: I think that it is _____ for people today to learn about the past.

Step 4

Complete the response using your outline from above.

    I think that _____.

First, _____.

For example, _____

_____.

Also, _____

_____.

Secondly, _____.

For example, _____

_____.

In addition, _____

_____

_____.

In conclusion, _____.

Integrated - Civics and Government

Getting Ready to Write

A. Learn the words.

Key Vocabulary

voice	the right to express opinions
power	control over a place
represent	to speak or act for another person or group of people
useless	having no use or purpose

TOEFL® Vocabulary

mutually	for two people or groups equally
notion	an idea about something
reject	to refuse to accept something
perspective	a way of thinking about something
clause	a rule that says that something must be done

Reading Passage

B. Read the first part of a passage. Then answer the questions.

Athenian Democracy

In ancient Greece, the people of Athens used a unique type of government. Their system was called Athenian democracy. In it, all adults voted on almost everything. This system was mutually good for the government and the people. It helped Greece in two ways.

1. What is the main idea of the passage?

(A) How Athenian democracy was good

(B) How Athenian democracy developed

2. What do you think the rest of the passage will talk about? Write two or three ideas below.

_____

_____

Practice

Lecture

A. Listen to the first part of a lecture. Then answer the question. `Track 45`

What is the main idea of the lecture?

(A) How Athenians voted on wars

(B) Why Athenian democracy was bad

Note-taking

B. Read the full passage. Then listen to the full lecture. Take notes in the boxes below. `Track 46`

Athenian Democracy

In ancient Greece, the people of Athens used a unique type of government. Their system was called Athenian democracy. In it, all adults voted on almost everything. This system was mutually good for the government and the people. It helped Greece in two ways.

To begin, it let all adults have a voice in the government. It gave the power directly to the people. Thus, the government truly represented the people. Everyone felt like they had a voice.

In addition, people were able to vote on everything. If there was a new law, the citizens voted on it. Even the smallest things were voted on by the people. For this reason, laws were good for the largest number of citizens. The people could vote against any laws that would be bad for them.

Reading

Main idea: Athenian democracy was good for the government and the people.
Key points:
- It let all adults have _____
- People were able to _____

Lecture

Main idea: Athenian democracy was bad for the people of Greece.
Key points:
- Not all people _____
  - There were certain _____ that made people unable to vote.
  - If you lived near the city walls, you couldn't _____
- It is not a good thing to have people vote _____
  - It meant that people have to vote on _____
  - It is better to have _____ handle small laws.

C. Read the prompt.

Summarize the main points made in the lecture and explain how they differ from the main points in the reading passage.

D. Fill in the blanks of the sample response using phrases from the box. Use your notes to help you.

The reading says that _____ was good for the people of Greece. The author gives two reasons for believing this. First, it let all adults have _____ in the government. In addition, people were able to vote on everything.

_____ that this was not good for the people. First, not all people were _____ on all of the laws. There were certain clauses that made some people unable to vote. For example, people who lived close to _____ couldn't vote on things having to do with war. Second, it isn't a good thing to have people vote on everything. It meant that people had to vote even on _____. It is better to have the government do that for the people.

a voice	the city walls
useless things	allowed to vote
The lecture says	Athenian democracy

E. Fill in the blanks with the correct words.

mutually   notion   reject   perspective   clause

1. Many legal documents have a _____ stating the rules of the agreement.
2. Many people _____ the idea that coffee is good for your health.
3. Depending on a person's _____, many laws can seem helpful or harmful.
4. The agreement was _____ beneficial; both people involved were able to solve their problems.
5. The _____ that the Earth is warming is becoming more widely accepted by people around the world.

Test

Step 1

Read the passage. Then listen to the lecture. Take notes in the boxes below. Track 47

Plato

The Greek philosopher Plato often wrote on the topic of government. In Plato's time, many people searched for the perfect form of government. Most agreed that a ruler must be good. Many disagreed on what good was. Plato believed a good ruler must come in the form of a philosopher-king. He believed this type of person was good for two reasons.

First, he believed only philosophers fully understood the world. They had knowledge that others did not. Thus, only they were fit to rule. Knowledge was the greatest good for Plato. Those with the most knowledge were good.

In addition, Plato believed that good came from doing good things. To be good, a king had to do good things for his people. For Plato, good people did these things naturally. In essence, there were good and bad people who could not change. The philosopher-king was always good. Therefore, he would naturally do good things.

Reading

Main idea: Plato believed the best ruler was a philosopher-king.
Key points:
- Only philosopher-kings _____
- Plato believed that good came from _____

Lecture

Main idea: Plato and Aristotle agreed that rulers must be good, but disagreed on

_____

Key points:
- Like Plato, Aristotle thought _____ was good.
  - Aristotle thought that it needed to be _____
  - Knowledge should be used to _____
- Aristotle also thought a good ruler should _____
  - For Aristotle, people did good things because _____
  - There weren't any people that were _____

Step 2

Read and listen to the prompt. Track 48

Summarize the main points made in the lecture and explain how they differ from the main points in the reading passage.

Step 3

Complete the outline using your notes from Step 1.

Topic: The best type of ruler according to Plato and Aristotle.

A. The reading says that the best ruler is a _____

    1. Only philosopher-kings _____

    2. Plato believed that good came from _____

B. The lecture says that Plato and Aristotle agreed that _____,
but disagreed on _____

    1. Like Plato, Aristotle thought _____

        • He thought that it needed to be _____

        • Knowledge should be used to _____

    2. Also like Plato, Aristotle thought _____

        • For Aristotle, people did good things because _____

        • There weren't any people that were _____

Conclusion: In that way, Aristotle was _____ from Plato.

Step 4

Complete the response using your outline from Step 3.

>   The reading and the lecture discuss _____
> _____.
> The reading says _____.
> Only philosopher-kings _____.
> Plato believed that good came from _____.
>   The lecture says that Plato and Aristotle _____
> _____.
> Like Plato, Aristotle thought _____.
> He thought that it needed to be _____.
> Knowledge should be used to _____.
> Second, Aristotle, like Plato, thought _____.
> For Aristotle, people did good things because _____.
> In addition, there weren't any people that were _____.
>   In conclusion, the lecture says that Plato and Aristotle _____.

Check-up

Fill in the blanks with the correct words.

value	college	plenty	point
voice	power	represent	useless

1. The _____ of studying is to be prepared for tests.
2. The _____ of gold is steadily increasing.
3. The _____ in most countries is given to a group of people called the government.
4. People in democracies choose someone to be their _____ in government.
5. A new product will certainly fail if consumers find it to be _____.
6. Many people want to attend _____ after high school.
7. If you travel in the desert, you should take _____ of water.
8. Power of Attorney is something that gives a person the ability to _____ someone else.

[12]

Getting Ready to Write

A. Learn the words.

Key Vocabulary

character	the combination of traits and features that define a person or a thing
image	the way something is seen
stuck	unable to move
ruin	to break

TOEFL® Vocabulary

conversely	oppositely
maintain	to continue something
construct	to build
constant	not changing
unrelated	not connected or sharing a relationship

B. Read the prompt. Then answer the questions.

Describe an experience when you visited a city.

1. What city did you visit?
I visited _____.

2. Why did you visit that city?
I visited that city because _____.

3. What did you like about that city?
I liked _____.

4. Did you see historic or modern buildings in the city?
I saw _____.

Practice

A. Read the question.

Do you agree or disagree with the following statement?

> Cities should repair their old and historic buildings rather than replace them with new and modern ones.

Use specific reasons and examples to support your answer.

Sample Response 1

B. Read the sample response. Then answer the question.

I think that cities should fix their old and historic buildings. This is better than replacing them with new ones. First, old buildings give a city its character. They make the city unique. They also tell you about its history. Many people visit cities just to see their old buildings. On the contrary, new buildings are the same all over the world. When you replace historic buildings with modern buildings, you make your city look just like all the other cities in the world. Second, old buildings are usually better built than new ones. In fact, many new buildings are poor quality. This is true in my town. For example, we had a storm that ruined many modern buildings. However, none of the old buildings were damaged. Clearly, they do not construct new buildings well. People made old buildings better. Therefore, it is better to repair historic buildings than replace them with new ones.

Which side of the statement does the response take?
(A) Agree   (B) Disagree

Outline

C. Complete the outline for the response.

Topic: Cities should _____.
  A. Old buildings give a city _____
     1. They make the city unique and tell _____
     2. Many people visit cities just to _____
  B. Old buildings are usually better _____
     1. Many new buildings _____
     2. People made old _____
Conclusion: It is better to _____ than replace them with _____.

D. Underline the transitional words or phrases in the sample response.

E. Read the sample response. Then answer the question.

I think that cities should replace their old buildings with new ones. There are two reasons. The first one is that it is too expensive to maintain old buildings. They are a constant problem. On the other hand, new buildings are not. They are built with the newest technology. Therefore, they are easier to maintain. Similarly, because they are constructed from better technology, they will have fewer problems than old buildings. That saves money. It can be used for other things. Second, new buildings look better. They fit with modern styles. They also show people that the city is not stuck in the past. Conversely, a city full of old buildings looks old-fashioned and ugly. They are unrelated to the city's future. Replacing old buildings is a good way to improve a city's image. In conclusion, I think that all cities should replace their old buildings with new ones. In fact, they should do it as soon as possible.

Which side of the statement does the response take?

(A) Agree   (B) Disagree

F. Complete the outline for the response.
Topic: Cities should _____.
A. It is too expensive to _____
   1. Old buildings are a _____
   2. New buildings are constructed using better technology, so they will have _____
   _____
B. New buildings _____
   1. They fit with _____ and show _____
   2. Replacing old buildings is a good way to _____
Conclusion: I think that all cities should replace their old buildings with new ones.

G. Underline the transitional words or phrases in the sample response.

H. Fill in the blanks with the correct words.

constant	construct	conversely	maintain	unrelated

1. It is important to _____ your car's engine so that it lasts a long time.
2. The color of a car is _____ to its performance.
3. My aunt is very tall; _____, my uncle is quite short.
4. They are going to _____ a new library at my school next year.
5. His visits to his grandparents are as _____ as the tides.

Test

Step 1

Do you agree or disagree with the following statement?

Cities should repair their old and historic buildings rather than replace them with new and modern ones.

Use specific reasons and examples to support your answer.

Step 2

I _____ with the statement.

Step 3

Topic: Cities _____ repair their old buildings.

A: _____

    1. _____

    2. _____

B. _____

    1. _____

    2. _____

Conclusion: That's why I think that cities _____ repair their old buildings.

Step 4

    I think that _____.

First, _____

_____.

For example, _____.

Furthermore, _____

_____.

Second, _____.

For example, _____

_____.

That's why I think _____.

Integrated - Communication

Getting Ready to Write

A. Learn the words.

Key Vocabulary

parrot	a brightly colored bird that can be taught to speak
combine	to put different things together
yield	to produce
sign language	a language that uses hand motions to make words

TOEFL® Vocabulary

feat	an impressive thing that someone does
exhibit	to show a particular thing or things
symbol	something that is used to represent something else
reinforce	to support an idea or argument by making it stronger
monitor	to watch something in order to find out something about it

Reading Passage

B. Read the first part of a passage. Then answer the questions.

Language

Learning language has long been thought to be too hard a feat for animals. After all, only humans seem to use language. Yet some animals have been able to learn to communicate with language. For an animal to learn language, it must exhibit two things.

1. What is the main idea of the passage?

    (A) Signs that an animal can learn language

    (B) Two kinds of animal communication

2. What do you think the rest of the passage will talk about? Write two or three ideas below.

_____

_____

Practice

A. Listen to the first part of a lecture. Then answer the question. `Track 49`

What is the main idea of the lecture?

(A) The steps of teaching animals to communicate

(B) How a study supports animals learning language

B. Read the full passage. Then listen to the full lecture. Take notes in the boxes below. `Track 50`

Language

Learning language has long been thought to be too hard a feat for animals. After all, only humans seem to have language at all. Yet some animals have been able to learn to communicate with language. For an animal to learn language, it must exhibit two things.

For one, it must be able to use words in some way. Repeating words, like a parrot does, is not language. The parrot only repeats sounds. It does not express feelings with words. However, some animals have learned to use words and symbols to express feelings.

The second thing animals must do to use language is combine words to form new thoughts. In other words, they cannot simply know what the correct word for a thing is. They must combine words together to create complete thoughts. Some animals have also been able to do this. These two things reinforce the idea that animals can learn language.

Reading

Main idea: Animals must do two things in order to learn language.
Key points:
- An animal must be able to _____ in some way.
- Animals must also _____ to form new thoughts.

Lecture

Main idea: A study of a chimp named Washoe proved that animals are able to learn language.
Key points:
- To learn language, an animal must _____
  - It must use certain words without _____
  - Washoe learned how to use over _____
- Washoe learned how to put _____
  - She came up with her own _____
  - She learned how to say these things _____

C. Read the prompt.

Summarize the main points made in the lecture and explain how they support the main points in the reading passage.

Sample Response

D. Fill in the blanks of the sample response using phrases from the box. Use your notes to help you.

The reading says that animals can _____ if they can do two things. First, an animal must be able to use words in some way. _____, it must be able to combine words to form new thoughts.

The lecture _____ by describing a study in which a chimp named Washoe learned sign language. _____ two things that Washoe did that support the idea that animals can learn language. First, animals must be able to use words. They must be able to use words without being told to do so. Washoe learned how to use over 250 different words. Washoe also learned how to _____ to make new thoughts. She came up with her own names for different things. She learned how to say these things _____.

combine words	The speaker describes
on her own	In addition
learn language	supports the reading

TOEFL® Vocabulary Practice

E. Fill in the blanks with the correct words.

feat   exhibit   symbol   reinforce   monitor

1. Many animals _____ a desire to learn new abilities taught by humans.

2. When an animal is sick, owners should _____ it closely and note any changes in behavior.

3. In sign language, a closed fist is the _____ for the letter "s."

4. Learning to sit when a human commands it is a(n) _____ that some dogs struggle to learn.

5. To make a good argument, you should _____ your opinions with facts or examples.

Test

Step 1

Read the passage. Then listen to the lecture. Take notes in the boxes below. `Track 51`

> ### Animals and Language
>
> Many studies have supported the idea that animals can learn language. But can animals learn writing? For animals, writing is a feat even more difficult than speaking. Yet some people believe that it is possible. There are two reasons to believe that animals can learn to write.
>
> First, studies have proven that animals can learn language. This is the first step in learning to write. Just as children first learn to say words and then to write, some animals can learn to do the same. After learning language, they can then begin to develop writings skills.
>
> Also, animals can learn symbols. Some animals have learned sign language. Sign language uses symbols to represent words. Other symbols can be written. If animals learn these symbols, they can also learn to write them. Thus, they have learned to write language.

Reading

Main idea: Animals can learn how to write language.
Key points:
- Studies have proven that animals can _____
- Also, animals can learn _____

Lecture

Main idea: Kanzi the bonobo learned how to write.
Key points:
- He first had to learn _____
  - Kanzi learned _____ called _____
  - In the woods, he touched _____ and then made a fire.
- He then learned how to _____
  - At one point, Kanzi wanted to _____
  - He took a piece of chalk and _____

Step 2

Read and listen to the prompt. `Track 52`

Summarize the main points made in the lecture and explain how they support the main points in the reading passage.

Step 3

Complete the outline using your notes from Step 1.

Topic: Whether animals can learn to write language.

A. The reading says that animals can learn how _____

    1. Studies have proven that _____

    2. Also, animals can learn _____

B. The lecture supports the reading by saying that Kanzi _____

    1. He first had to learn _____

        • Kanzi learned _____

        • In the woods, he touched _____

    2. He then learned how to _____

        • At one point, Kanzi wanted to _____

        • He took a piece of chalk and _____

Conclusion: Kanzi learned how to both _____

        and _____.

Step 4

Complete the response using your outline from Step 3.

    The reading and the lecture discuss _____.

The reading says that animals _____.

Studies have proven that _____.

Also, animals can learn _____.

    The lecture supports the reading by saying that _____.

First, he had to learn _____.

Kanzi learned _____.

In the woods, he touched _____.

Second, he learned how to _____.

At one point, Kanzi wanted to _____.

He took a piece of chalk and _____.

    Thus, the lecture supports the reading because it says that Kanzi learned how to both _____ and _____.

Check-up

Fill in the blanks with the correct words.

ruin	image	stuck	character
parrot	combine	yield	sign language

1. While a(n) _____ is able to say words, it does not know what they mean.

2. If you behave badly, you will hurt your _____.

3. When animal experiments _____ surprising results, the researchers often repeat the experiment to check their results.

4. If you are not careful with delicate technology, you could _____ it.

5. If you throw chewing gum on the ground, it may get _____ to someone's shoe.

6. An animal can only be said to use language when it is able to _____ different words together.

7. The bright lights and tall buildings of New York give the city its _____.

8. _____ was invented as a way for deaf people to communicate.

[Review 2]

Step 1

Read the question.

Do you agree or disagree with the following statement?

Reading is better for children than playing video games.

Use specific reasons and examples to support your answer.

Step 2

State your opinion.

I _____ with the statement.

Step 3

Write an outline for your essay that will support your opinion.

Topic: Reading is _____ than playing video games.

A. _____

    1. _____

    2. _____

       _____

B. _____

    1. _____

    2. _____

Conclusion: This is why I think _____.

Step 4

Complete the response using your outline from above.

I think that reading _____.

To begin, I think _____.

I think that _____

_____.

For example, _____

_____.

I also believe that _____.

I feel that _____

_____.

This is why I think _____.

Step 1

Read the passage. Then listen to the lecture. Take notes in the boxes below. **Track 53**

Real Life in Fiction

Fiction is a kind of story that is not true. Many people think fiction is always about fake events. However, the plot in a fiction book can sometimes use real people or events. Authors use people or events from their own lives. They often write about their own lives in two ways.

First, they can use real people from their lives. Some authors make a character using themselves. They often pick a new name. They also sometimes use people they knew from the past. Many times, authors can create credible characters this way. Some fiction characters do not seem real. Conversely, a real person from an author's life will seem more real in a book.

Authors also use real events from their lives. It is common for an author to write about his or her life as a child. Other authors favor writing about the life of a friend. Again, they change names and details to make it fiction. In either case, real life can be very inspiring to fiction writers.

Reading

Main idea: Authors often create fiction stories by _____
Key points:
  • Authors often use _____ to make fictional characters.
  • To create a plot, authors sometimes use _____

Lecture

Main idea: Mark Twain created *The Adventures of Tom Sawyer* by writing about

_____

Key points:
  • Twain used _____ to make the
    characters in the book.
    - Tom Sawyer, the main character, is based on _____
    - To make good characters, Twain decided to use _____
  • Twain based the book's events on _____
    - The book's story is about _____
    - A scene where Tom's friends paint a fence was _____

Step 2

Read and listen to the prompt. **Track 54**

Summarize the main points made in the lecture and explain how they support the main points in the reading passage.

Step 3

Topic: The reading and the lecture discuss authors who use real events in fiction writing.

A. The reading discusses two ways that fiction writers _____

_____

    1. Authors often use _____ to make fictional characters.

    2. To create a plot, authors sometimes use _____

B. The lecture _____ by discussing how Mark Twain wrote *The Adventures of Tom Sawyer.*

    1. Twain used _____ to make the characters in the book.

       • Tom Sawyer, the main character, is based on _____

       • To make good characters, Twain decided to use _____

    2. Twain based the book's events on _____

       • The book's story is about _____

       • A scene where Tom's friends paint a fence was _____

Conclusion: The lecture _____ the reading by _____

_____ .

Step 4

    The reading and the lecture both discuss _____

_____ .

The reading discusses two ways that _____

_____ .

Firstly, authors often use _____ .

Secondly, to create a plot, authors sometimes use _____ .

    The lecture _____ by discussing _____

_____ .

The speaker says that Twain used _____

_____ .

Tom Sawyer, the main character, is based on _____ .

To make good characters, Twain decided to use _____ .

In addition, the speaker says that Twain based the book's events on _____

_____ .

The book's story is about _____ .

A scene where Tom's friends paint a fence was _____ .

    In conclusion, the lecture _____

_____ .

Step 1

Read the passage. Then listen to a lecture. Take notes in the boxes below. Track 55

Media and the Public Interest

The media are present in all of our lives. From TV to newspapers, we all interact with the media every day. But what are the motives of the media? Why do they show the programs they do? The media act in the public interest. That is, the main goal of the media is to please the greatest number of people. This is evident from the following two facts.

First, entertainment media show what people want to see. This is exhibited best in TV programming. TV networks choose the shows that people like most. This is because they want their watchers to have a constant selection of good shows. They choose good shows to make the public happy.

Second, the media reports the news that people need to see the most. Getting vital news to the public is the most important thing in journalism. Thus, the media picks the most essential news stories to report. That way, they please as many people as possible.

Reading

Main idea: The goal of the media is to _____
Key points:
- The entertainment media show _____
- The media report the news that people _____

Lecture

Main idea: The aim of the media is _____
Key points:
- TV networks show things that _____
  - The only reason for showing commercials is _____
  - Commercials do not serve _____
- The point of _____ is only to make money.
  - News stations and newspapers need to _____
  - So they pick news that will _____ instead of _____ people.

Step 2

Read and listen to the prompt. Track 56

Summarize the main points made in the lecture and explain how they cast doubt on the main points in the reading passage.

Step 3

Complete the outline using your notes from Step 1.

Topic: The reading and the lecture discuss whether the media serve the public interest.
A. The reading suggests that the media _____
   1. The entertainment media show _____
   2. The media report the news that people _____
B. The lecture _____ by offering two arguments.
   1. TV networks show things that _____
      • The only reason for showing commercials is _____
      • Commercials do not serve _____
   2. The point of _____ is only to make money.
      • News stations and newspapers need to _____
      • So they pick news that will _____ instead of _____ people.
Conclusion: The lecture _____ with the reading by saying that
_____.

Step 4

Complete the response using your outline from Step 3.

   The reading and the lecture discuss _____.
The author of the passage says the media _____
_____. The author first says that entertainment media show
_____.
Next, the author says that the media report _____
_____.
   The lecture _____ by offering _____.
First, TV networks only show things that _____.
The only reason they show commercials is _____.
Therefore, commercials do not _____.
The speaker also says that the point of _____.
Newspapers and news stations _____.
So they pick news that _____.
   In conclusion, the lecture _____
_____.

Step 1

Read the question.

Do you agree or disagree with the following statement?

People who send many text messages, instant messages, and email have bad spelling.

Use specific reasons and examples to support your answer.

Step 2

State your opinion.

I _____ with the statement.

Step 3

Write an outline for you essay that will support your opinion.

Topic: People who send many text messages, instant messages, and email _____
 bad spelling.

A. _____

    1. _____

    2. _____

B. _____

    1. _____

    2. _____

Conclusion: This is why I think that _____.

Step 4

Complete the response using your outline from above.

I think that people _____
_____.
First, I think _____.
I believe that _____
_____.
When I send email, _____
_____.
Secondly, I think _____.
In my opinion, _____.
For example, _____.
This is why I think that _____.

Writing 2
Worksheets

Unit 1 Worksheet: To-infinitives as Nouns

A to-infinitive is a noun form of a verb. It refers to the act of doing a certain action. As such, its form does not change in relation to tense or subject. It can be used as a subject, object, or complement. As a subject, it comes before the main verb of the sentence. As an object, it takes the direct action of the verb. As a complement, it completes the meaning of another part of the sentence.

Subject
To play tennis is John's favorite afternoon activity. To think otherwise is a mistake.

Object
John wants to play tennis this afternoon.   My dogs try to cheer me up.

Complement
But their only jobs are to eat, sleep, and play.   We like our dogs to watch TV with us.

A. Write an S beside sentences that use a to-infinitive as a subject and an O beside sentences that use a to-infinitive as an object.

1. The children want to go to the park. _____
2. To be a pilot is Lisa's dream. _____
3. She refused to study for the exam, and she did poorly on it. _____
4. We can't afford to go to a movie tonight. _____
5. To treat others with respect is what all people should do. _____
6. To think otherwise is a mistake. _____
7. My dogs will try to cheer me up. _____
8. With a bad leader, fewer people wanted to fight. _____

B. Put the to-infinitive into the correct position in each sentence.

1. _____ we also take _____ them _____ on picnics with us. (to go)
2. _____ it is sad not _____ about _____ improving your relationship with your family. (to care)
3. _____ his job is _____ the horses on _____ the farm. (to feed)
4. _____ its military properly was _____ something that _____ Rome failed at. (to manage)
5. _____ pets as important _____ as other family members is _____ not good. (to treat)
6. _____ with a bad leader, fewer _____ people wanted _____. (to fight)
7. _____ they began _____ the value _____ of their money. (to reduce)
8. _____ attacked many times can _____ weaken a country's _____ infrastructure. (to be)

C. Complete the sentences with an infinitive and information about you.

1. I like _____ when I am really hungry.
2. _____ is my favorite thing to do on a cold winter day.
3. My chores at home are _____.

Unit 2 Worksheet: Gerunds

A gerund is another noun form of a verb. It refers to the act of doing a certain action. As such, its form does not change in relation to tense or subject. It can be used as a subject, object, or complement. As a subject, it comes before the main verb of the sentence. As an object, it takes the direct action of the verb. As a complement, it completes the meaning of another part of the sentence.

Subject
Loaning money to friends requires trust.
Repaying borrowed money is important for maintaining trust between friends.

Object
My sister likes altering old clothes to match modern styles.
We enjoy skiing every winter.

Complement
Our teacher recommends helping less fortunate people.
The best exercises include swimming, walking, and skiing.

A. Write an O beside sentences that use a gerund as an object and a C beside sentences that use a gerund as a complement.

1. Some builders like using designs from history. _____
2. This will keep the hot air from circulating through the church. _____
3. I think that borrowing money from a friend is not a good idea. _____
4. Feelings can become tense if repaying the loan becomes difficult. _____
5. Complete knowledge of climate is necessary for designing suitable buildings. _____
6. Most people are afraid of speaking in front of a group of strangers. _____
7. Try eating fewer fried foods and exercising more. _____
8. Architecture never stops evolving. _____

B. Put the gerund into the correct position in each sentence.

1. _____ in different _____ climates can change _____ a design. (building)
2. _____ some builders like _____ designs from _____ history. (using)
3. _____ to borrow money is _____ awkward _____. (asking)
4. _____ from friends is _____ just not _____ in her nature. (stealing)
5. _____ one thing to consider is _____ different materials to _____ meet your purpose. (transforming)
6. _____ it is best to avoid _____ the class during a(n) _____ exam. (disrupting)
7. _____ you should consider _____ your loan _____ early. (repaying)
8. _____ could you gather _____ the materials for _____ the bread? (making)

C. Complete the sentences with a gerund and information about you.

1. I like _____ when I am really thirsty.
2. _____ is my favorite thing to do on a hot summer day.
3. I have a friend who hates _____.

Unit 3 Worksheet: Subject-Verb Agreement

In all sentences, the verb must agree with the subject. That is, the verb must be conjugated to match the form of the subject. Infinitives and gerunds both act as singular third-person nouns, so they take singular third-person verbs. If the sentence has a compound subject made up of two or more infinitives or gerunds, the verb should agree with the plural third-person form.

Finding a cure for an illness requires years of research and testing.
Treating an illness and curing it are not the same thing.
To give is more rewarding than to receive.
To talk about helping and to actually help are two different things.

A. **Circle the correct form of the verb to complete the sentence.**

1. Just seeing the pretty flowers (was / were) fun.
2. To be polite and to have respect for elders (is / are) two things lacking in most children today.
3. To pay attention to teachers (is / are) important for students.
4. Listening to what adults advise (helps / help) children develop maturity.
5. Pretending to be good but acting badly (is / are) worse than just being naughty.
6. To find new plants (is / are) one part of botany that most people enjoy.
7. Opening big gardens filled with many plants (attract / attracts) a lot of visitors.
8. Cataloging plants (take / takes) patience and concentration.

B. **Complete the sentences with the correct gerund or infinitive from the box.**

borrowing	getting	pretending
to have	to hold	to facilitate

1. _____ a job is just one part of the transition from childhood to adulthood.
2. _____ a door open for others and to say thank you are both polite acts.
3. _____ fun and break the rules is part of a child's nature.
4. _____ to be someone you're not requires careful attention to detail.
5. _____ international expansion is just one of your duties on this job.
6. Lending and _____ money are everyday business practices.

C. **Answer the questions. Use gerunds in two sentences and to-infinitives in two sentences.**

1. What activity requires a lot of concentration?

   _____

2. What two activities are very difficult to do?

   _____

3. What are your two favorite school activities?

   _____

4. What activity needs a lot of strength?

   _____

Unit 4 Worksheet: To-infinitives for Purpose

The to-infinitive form can also be used to explain the purpose of the action in the sentence. *In order* can also come before the to-infinitive to more clearly emphasize the purpose.

Carbon dating is used (in order) to find out the ages of many things.
Scientists use it (in order) to estimate how old artifacts are.
Two things can be done (in order) to make carbon dating better.
I think many people join a group (in order) to make friends.

A. Put a check (✓) beside the sentences that use a to-infinitive to indicate purpose.

1. Some scientists use chemicals in order to preserve items they don't want to decay. _____
2. The group used teamwork to accomplish their goals. _____
3. The coach likes the team to practice for two hours each evening. _____
4. Scientists can look at tree rings in order to calculate a tree's age. _____
5. All living things begin to decay after they die. _____
6. The whole team wants to have dinner at that restaurant. _____
7. However, scientists can use other chemicals to remove the bad ones. _____
8. Calibration uses other living things in order to find past rates of decay. _____

B. Complete the sentences with the to-infinitive form of a word from the box.

win	fix	learn	meet
make	enter	treat	find

1. They can use carbon dating _____ the carbon level through the tree's life.
2. There are two things that can be done in order _____ carbon dating better.
3. All the players on the team must unite in order _____ a championship.
4. Some people think chemicals can be used _____ problems with dating.
5. I decided to join the soccer team in high school _____ new people.
6. Doctors sometimes use radiation _____ patients with serious illnesses.
7. Regardless of their advantages, rich students still must work hard in order _____ a good university.
8. Archaeologists examine artifacts _____ more about past cultures.

C. Answer the questions with sentences that include a to-infinitive for purpose.

1. Why do you study English?

   _____

2. Why do you brush your teeth?

   _____

3. Why should you exercise every day?

   _____

Unit 5 Worksheet: Noun Clauses with *That*

A noun clause is a part of a sentence that includes both a noun and a verb. Though a noun clause can be used as a subject, it is most commonly used as an object or complement. Many noun clauses begin with the word *that*. When used as an object or complement, *that* is optional.

Subject
That you speak Mandarin will help you when you visit China.
That you have little free time is of no importance to me.

Object
I think (that) volunteering teaches young people responsibility.
My parents like (that) I study in the library every day after school.

Complement
They meet people (that) they didn't even know were there.
The dog (that) my neighbors just got is very friendly.

A. Underline the noun clause in each sentence. Then write S if it is used as a subject or C if it is used as a complement.

1. Most people invest in businesses that they can trust. _____
2. That he is the boss's nephew surely helped him get the job. _____
3. That he rebels against his teachers now will not help him in the future. _____
4. The girl that I met last night volunteers at the seniors' center. _____
5. We need to come up with some healthy activities that teens can engage in. _____
6. That you're learning to run a business now will be a great benefit in the future. _____
7. That she is so young is not relevant to her ability to do the job. _____
8. The movies that he adapted from her books generated millions of dollars. _____

B. Match the sentence to the noun clause that correctly completes it.

1. The books _____ I found to be quite boring.
2. _____ means she will be successful.
3. The owners hope _____.
4. The revenue generated from the sales of these flowers will be donated to the charity _____.

(A) that integrating new rides will make the theme park more successful
(B) that my teacher regarded highly
(C) that my grandmother founded
(D) that she never loses sight of her objective

C. Complete the sentences with a noun clause starting with *that*.

1. I hope _____.
2. _____ makes me different than most people.
3. The food _____ was really delicious.
4. There is a new movie coming out _____.

Unit 6 Worksheet: Noun Clauses after Dummy Subjects

A dummy subject (*It*) is used to express an opinion about a condition. A *that* noun clause is often used as a complement to explain the opinion or condition. The *that* clause is the logical subject of the sentence in this case, but the *It* is the actual, structural subject.

Examples
That she be on time is important.   It is important that she be on time.

In the sentence above, *That she be on time* is the subject. In the second sentence, *It* becomes the subject. The form of the second sentence is far more common in English. It emphasizes the opinion (*important*) over the condition (*she be on time*).

A. Put a check (✓) beside the sentences that use a dummy subject.

1. It is sad that many people in cities do not care about conservation. _____
2. It is that idea that led to the theory of plate tectonics. _____
3. It is over there, beside the park bench. _____
4. That they teach people about nature is the reason we are here today. _____
5. It should be a crime when animal populations are endangered. _____
6. That people still continue to hunt them is at the heart of the issue. _____
7. That we should be more aware of the damage we cause to nature is the point I am trying to make. _____
8. Finally, it is important that people understand why it is necessary to conserve nature. _____

B. Rewrite the sentences so that they use a dummy subject.

1. That animals be free to roam in nature is better.

   _____

2. That the animals ran away was really sad.

   _____

3. That we protect animals regardless of the cost is important.

   _____

4. That many people did not know it was possible for plates to move is interesting.

   _____

C. Complete the sentences with your own information and opinions.

1. It is important that parents _____.
2. It is sad when people _____.
3. It is necessary that students _____.
4. It is frustrating when _____.

Unit 7 Worksheet: Noun Clauses with *Wh-* Words, *If*, and *Whether*

Noun clauses often begin with *wh-* words to give specific kinds of information. They can also begin with *if* or *whether* to show a condition. The phrase *or not* often comes at the end of an *if/whether* clause. *Or not* can also be placed immediately after *whether*, but not after *if*.

The government knew what they had to do to protect non-smokers.
Many of the heroes who children now look up to first appeared in legends.
A law of this importance would only be successful if society embraces it.
We can't be sure if the statistics are reliable or not.
I always wondered whether or not the ban on smoking was meant to teach us something.

A. Complete the sentences with the correct *wh-* word.

1. Therefore, writers use myths to portray _____ a world would be like with no moral grounding.
2. I don't know _____ the students examining those legends are.
3. Do you know _____ it is evident that society realized the dangers of cigarettes?
4. I have always wondered _____ legends came from.
5. Do you remember _____ the man who wrote about myths and legends was?
6. Clearly, _____ children see around them influences their behavior.
7. I still can't imagine _____ people smoke.
8. I can't understand _____ purpose legends and myths serve.

B. Use the word given to complete the sentences based on the questions.

1. Did we make reservations in the non-smoking section?
   We don't know _____. (if)
2. Did I hear that myth before?
   I'm not sure _____. (whether)
3. Is cancer the leading cause of death?
   She can't remember _____. (if)
4. Does he want me to invite non-smoking guests?
   I wonder _____. (whether)

C. Rewrite the sentences by adding *or not* to the noun clauses.

1. I wonder whether people know the dangers of second-hand smoke.

   _____

2. I don't know if the smoking ban is viewed by smokers to be a tragedy.

   _____

3. I can't decide whether I want to quit smoking.

   _____

4. Whether the big tobacco companies had a motive is not important.

   _____

Unit 8 Worksheet: Tense—Simple Past & Present Perfect

The simple past is used to talk about an action or event that began and ended in the past. The present perfect is used to talk about an action or event that happened in the past, but is still important in the present.

Simple Past
It took me two hours to drive to work this morning.
In 2003, I commuted to work every day.

Present Perfect
I think it might take us two hours to travel ten miles because the traffic has been bad lately.
It has taken me two hours to drive this far, and I still have thirty kilometers to go.

A. **Write SP beside sentences that use simple past tense and PP beside sentences that use present perfect tense.**

   1. In fact, it's so close that he has started riding his bike to work. _____
   2. I used to think that there was no other alternative. _____
   3. I rode my bicycle to work every day in the summer of 2001. _____
   4. I have had the same car for twelve years. _____
   5. The fuel has never reached its mass appeal potential. _____
   6. Scientists jumped at the chance to apply for the grant last year. _____
   7. The time I have spent traveling to work recently is far less than before. _____
   8. I have grappled with the prospect of an oil-free world, but I don't see it happening anytime soon. _____

B. **Complete the sentences with the correct tense of the verbs given.**

   1. Last week, a renowned scientist _____ that ethanol cannot be a substitute for fossil fuels. (say)
   2. But recently, another well-known researcher _____ better ways to make ethanol. (design)
   3. Oil companies _____ little luck in developing the new technology up to this point in time. (have)
   4. I _____ on finding a sustainable energy source, but have not succeeded so far. (work)
   5. We _____ to a convention on renewable energy last weekend. (go)
   6. The convention _____ booked solid for two years running. (be)
   7. After switching to ethanol, she _____ $400 last year. (save)
   8. At my last job, the time I _____ driving to and from work made me exhausted. (spend)

C. **Answer the questions with sentences that include the simple past or present perfect tense.**

   1. Did you use any fossil fuels yesterday? What for?

   _____

   2. Have you ever traveled to school by bicycle instead of by bus?

   _____

   3. How long have you lived in the city you live in now?

   _____

   4. When did you start studying English?

   _____

Unit 9 Worksheet: Basic Complex Sentences

A complex sentence is made up of an independent clause connected to one or more dependant clauses. A complex sentence can have a subordinator such as *when, because, if*, or *whereas*. If the subordinator is at the beginning of the complex sentence, a comma (,) is used to separate the dependant and independent clauses. When a subordinator is in the middle of complex sentence, it does not need a comma.

What happens when you get fewer than eight hours of sleep?
When you read a newspaper or book, you can trust the information.
We can trust the information because we know it is reliable.
If you could trust the Internet, we wouldn't have these questions.

A. **Underline the dependant clause in each sentence. Add a comma where one is needed.**

1. When someone asserts something is correct on the Internet it is up to the reader to second guess the assertion.
2. Journalism can be a rewarding career choice if it is taken seriously and respected.
3. If an Internet blog provides an account of something it shouldn't necessarily be taken as fact.
4. I know what I read to be true because the information came from a news website.
5. This is a good thing because it makes it easier for people to talk with each other.

B. **Choose the correct subordinator to complete the sentences.**

1. First, people didn't seem as alert or as smart (when / whereas) they got four hours of sleep.
2. (When / Before) you read a newspaper or book, you can trust the information.
3. (If / Because) people don't document where their information comes from, it is hard to know if the material is reliable.
4. Be certain the facts provided are correct (before / if) you accept information from the Internet.
5. (Because / After) anyone can write information on the Internet, the information might not be trustworthy.

C. **Complete the sentences with your own information.**

1. If I could change one thing about the Internet, I would _____

_____.

2. I usually read _____, whereas my parents usually read _____.

3. I enjoy _____ because _____.

4. I sometimes get angry when _____.

Unit 10 Worksheet: Tense in Time and First Conditional Clauses

A future time clause can start with *when*, *after*, and *before*. A time clause can be placed in front of or after the main clause. If a time clause is placed in front of the main clause, a comma (,) is put after the time clause. The verb stays in the simple present tense when the time clause refers to the future.

A first conditional clause is also known as an *if* clause. We use an *if* clause to express future time. The verb also stays in the simple present tense. An *if* clause can be placed in front of or after the main clause. When an *if* clause is placed in front of the main clause, a comma (,) is put after it.

Time clauses
When a new computer comes out a month from now, how much faster do you think it will be?
After the expected results, we will begin our next endeavor.

If clauses
If I have a guideline, I can get started right away.
Philanthropy is only successful if organizations being invested in are credible.

A. Underline the time clause in each sentence.

1. And when this happens, the law won't be true anymore.
2. After we create a camera and put it on the market, we begin creating one to replace it.
3. We should test the transistors before we ship them overseas.
4. When one computer gets faster, that means there are more to follow.
5. Our proportion of market share climbed after we introduced the improved model.
6. Before you go any further, you should research last year's trends.
7. You should buy a new computer after they introduce their new designs.
8. When this camera is launched, we will see gains in our stock price.

B. Complete the sentences with the correct *if* clause.

If the company fails,	If we work hard on our company,
if I become rich.	if we can't figure out how to fix these chips.

1. _____ it will be a success.
2. The new computer will be delayed _____.
3. I will be generous with my money _____.
4. _____ the blame will be placed solely on the investors.

C. Complete the sentences with your own information.

1. If the weather _____ this weekend, I will _____.

2. When I get hungry in the afternoon, I _____.

3. If I study a lot for an exam, _____.

4. When I don't get enough sleep, I _____.

Unit 11 Worksheet: Transitions for Logical Results

Transitions are words or phrases that connect the information in one sentence or section of a passage to that of another. One common usage of transitions is to indicate logical results. The following transitions can be used to indicate a logical result of preceding information: then, therefore, thus, as a result, for this/that reason(s). A comma (,) is placed after a transition.

Thus, the government truly represented the people.
Nobody lives that way anymore; therefore, knowing the past can't make any contribution to our lives today.

A. Put a check (✓) beside the sentences that use a transition to indicate logical results.

1. Therefore, he would naturally do good things. _____
2. The Greeks tried to create a society that was ruled by the people; thus, democracy was born. _____
3. They contain wisdom of former generations and give us a framework for how to live our lives. _____
4. After, power was permanently in the hands of the people. _____
5. For these reasons, democratic values were exported around the world. _____
6. First, turn left at the next street; then walk straight for five minutes. _____

B. Match the sentence or clause to the sentence or clause below that correctly completes it.

1. The law is created to provide the guidelines for how we live our lives.

   _____

2. A democratic society is useless if the government does not respect the law.

   _____

3. History shows examples of when democracies prospered and failed.

   _____

4. History not only documents the past, but it gives us a perspective on our culture.

   _____

Thus, you need to know about your history to understand your culture.
Therefore, in order to live well we need only to review the law.
Thus, the people must know when and how to assert their power.
For these reasons, I think it is very valuable for people today to learn about the past.

C. Complete the sentences with your own information.

1. _____; as a result, my parents were angry with me.

2. _____; therefore, my parents were proud of me.

3. _____; thus, I was very happy that day.

Unit 12 Worksheet: Transitions for Example, Emphasis, and Contrast

Transitions can be used for several purposes, not just to introduce logical results. Other purposes include introducing examples to clarify a point (*for example, for instance, namely, specifically, to illustrate*), emphasizing an argument or point (*even, indeed, in fact, of course, truly*), and contradicting an expectation or earlier point (*but, however, in spite of, on the one hand . . . on the other hand, nevertheless, nonetheless, in contrast, notwithstanding, on the contrary, still, yet*).

For example, we had a storm that ruined many modern buildings.
In fact, many new buildings are poor quality.
Some animals, however, have learned to use words and symbols to express feelings.

A. **Write EX beside the sentence if the transition is used to provide an example, E if it is used to show emphasis, and C if the transition is used to show contrast.**

1. Conversely, a city full of old buildings looks old-fashioned and ugly. _____
2. Clearly, they do not construct new buildings well. _____
3. Specifically, historic buildings give cities their unique character. _____
4. On the other hand, new buildings are not. _____
5. In contrast, new apartment buildings can be built with space for people to park their cars underground. _____
6. Indeed, that is why people want to go there. _____

B. **Circle the best transition to complete the sentence.**

1. Animals often communicate with body language. (Clearly / On the other hand), only humans seem to have language at all.
2. A huge storm blew through town last night. (For example / However), none of the old buildings were damaged.
3. I prefer chocolate ice cream; (conversely / similarly), my sister prefers vanilla.
4. There is very little originality to modern architecture. (On the contrary / In fact), new buildings are the same all over the world.

C. **Change the two sentences into one sentence using a transition.**

1. The new buildings were battered by the storm. None of the old buildings were damaged.

   _____

   _____

2. The life expectancy of a new building is relatively short. They don't construct buildings well.

   _____

   _____

3. Most people enjoy modern style architecture. I much prefer traditional buildings.

   _____

   _____

4. Many old apartment buildings were built before people had cars. New apartment buildings can be built with space for people to park their cars underground.

   _____

   _____

Writing Feedback and Evaluation Form

The response...	0	1	2	3	4
C O N T E N T — addresses the question or prompt well					
is organized					
has relevant details					
shows clear connections between ideas					
L A N G U A G E — uses accurate grammar					
uses appropriate vocabulary					
uses accurate spelling and punctuation					

Total: _____ /28

Basic Skills for the
TOEFL® iBT 2

Jeff Zeter

[Unit 1]

Practice

Page 12

W: Did the military ruin Rome? Yes, but not from *inside*. External military forces caused the fall of Rome. In fact, two groups caused it. (***Practice A ends.***) The first was the Persians. They attacked many areas from 200–300 CE, and Rome suffered a major defeat in 260 CE. Rome's leader was captured by the Persians. He became a servant to the Persian king. This hurt Rome. It lowered its confidence, for one. The troops were no longer as sure of their military. It also took a good leader away from Rome. Barbarians also attacked Rome many times. In fact, many groups invaded from northern Europe. One tribe, the Goths, attacked Rome many times. This weakened Rome's infrastructure. Troops were often fighting the Goths. It even hurt the economy. Goths often stole money and treasure. In time, the Romans just couldn't protect themselves. The empire fell.

Test

Page 14

M: A great leader can deal with any problem, right? We've seen how Rome's money problems affected its decline. But its political troubles were the real problem. All of Rome's problems were with its leader, rather than external problems like the Goths. Let me explain. Most rulers in Rome were chosen because they were strong leaders. But not Commodus. He was the son of the previous leader. He only became the leader because of his father. This was a mistake. He was not a good leader. The people didn't like him. He didn't have much political experience. And *he* really caused all of Rome's problems. A new problem arose one hundred years later. One of Rome's rulers split the empire. There was now a western half and an eastern half. It seemed like a good idea at the time. But it had two bad effects. A civil war started in 311 CE. This weakened the empire. It also allowed barbarians to invade. So politics, not money, made Rome fall.

[Unit 2]

Practice

Page 22

M: Many buildings use foreign designs. Countries often inspire other countries' buildings. But those designs often have to change. Let's look at churches in New Mexico. They were built to look like churches in Spain. But they had to transform for two reasons. (***Practice A ends.***) The first had to do with location. Spain and New Mexico have different climates. Spain is fairly mild. But New Mexico can be very hot. So the design changed when it moved from Spain to New Mexico. Spanish churches had windows covered with glass. New Mexican churches were not built with large windows. Doing this keeps the hot air from circulating through the church, which keeps it cool. Secondly, the churches used different materials. The Spanish churches were made of stone. But the builders in New Mexico didn't have stone. They did have plenty of dirt. So they built with mud. They used a design similar to the Spanish churches. But they had to change the materials they built with.

Test

Page 24

W: Many old buildings have designs that modern builders want to use. But designs often transform when used in modern times. Sometimes it's a small change. But, from time to time, they are altered in major ways. Let's take a look at two examples. First, buildings change when new materials are made. Modern buildings are much safer than older ones. That's because they did not use the strong metals we have today. For example, steel is a strong type of metal. Many new buildings use it. So a building made to look like a Greek building might use steel. It evolved to use modern materials. Second, some cultures have different styles. For example, the Greeks liked to decorate with symbols of leaves. Leaves were a popular symbol in Greece. But when a Greek design was used recently, symbols of corn were used. They thought this was a better symbol of modern life. So designs do change when used in a new place.

Transcript

[Unit 3]

Practice

Page 32

W: Who made the study of botany popular? Was it the common people? No, it wasn't. Botany became popular because of science. There are two reasons why this is true. (*Practice A ends.*) First, the comprehensive study of plants had many medical uses. Plants were used in cures. Students studied how plants could be used to treat illnesses. Only after that did botany make the transition from science to public hobby. Science made studying botany popular for many people. People wanted to see how plants could be used in medicine. Scientists created that interest. But there's a second reason too. Lots of scientists wanted to find every plant in the world. Many of them created systems to catalog plants. They wanted to find all of the plants in each group. Over time, the public joined in the search. They also wanted to find new plants. So interest from people studying botany was the main thing that made the public like it too. That's why it became popular.

Test

Page 34

M: It took a long while for botany to become a science. What finally made it transform? The answer is scientists, of course. Once scientists finally found it to be important, it became a true science. There are two things that happened to change the way people saw botany. First, universities had a role. The first gardens were meant for the public. People mostly used them to relax. Scientists wanted to *study* plants. So universities made their own gardens. This let them study plants and learn that botany was important. Second, scientists at first didn't see how botany could be used. Some used it for medical reasons. But one person changed all that. His name was Carl Linnaeus. He created a system to put plants in groups. After that, people wanted to find plants and put them in groups. Many scientists became involved in botany after that. Therefore, scientists made botany a true science.

[Unit 4]

Practice

Page 42

M: Carbon dating sounds good, but it has some problems. It's not very precise. Scientists can guess how old something is, but it is still just a guess. Let's look at two reasons that it isn't very exact. (*Practice A ends.*) Some people think that carbon has always decayed at the same definite rate. Well, it hasn't. It was very different in the past. It was much, much faster. So, really, there's no way to tell how long it used to take for carbon to decay. We can only know how long it takes now. This makes carbon dating flawed. There's another problem. It can only date things that are less than about 40,000 years old. Otherwise, there is hardly any carbon left at all. There's too little carbon to find its age. So it becomes a technique that can't be used in many studies.

Test

Page 44

W: There are lots of ways that people think carbon dating can be fixed. However, they won't work. Carbon dating is a process that can't be fixed. The two solutions are flawed. The first solution uses tree rings to make dating more precise. However, this has its own problems. First, not many trees have been alive for thousands of years. So we can't learn much about really old things with this method. Also, one tree only tells you about one place. Let's say you want to date something in Rome. You would have to study a tree from there too. It would also have to be older than the item. Sounds complex, right? Second, some people think chemicals can be used to fix the dating process. However, chemicals make dating less precise. Some scientists use chemicals to preserve items. These chemicals can change the results. Therefore, these two ideas cannot make carbon dating better.

[Unit 5]

Practice

Page 52

W: Many seasonal businesses do well. But they have to make some adjustments. A lot of things are different from normal businesses. One theme park in New York is only open in the summer. The owners make enough money to close the park in the winter. How can they be sure they make enough money? Let's find out. (*Practice A ends.*) First, making money is the main objective. They try not to spend money when the park is open. They make sure they don't spend more money than they make. And, of course, they sell tickets. The ticket sales must give them money to save for the winter. So the price must be high enough to make money. Second, they plan ahead. The park has a lot of rides and machines. Sometimes they break. So the park must plan to have money to fix them. They also have to pay taxes even when they're closed.

Test

Page 54

M: For a seasonal business, the revenue made in one season is not enough. But does that mean seasonal businesses can't work? Not at all. Many have found success by trying new things. Let's look at two merchants that have done very well. The first merchant did well by opening a new store. At first, the woman ran a landscaping business. During the winter, business was bad. So she needed a new way to make money in the winter. So she opened a store that sold holiday supplies. This gave her plenty of revenue in the winter. So she made money all year. The second merchant did well by adding new products to a store. A woman owned a store that sold outdoor furniture, but sales were bad in the colder seasons. So the owner started selling indoor products as well. That way, she still made plenty of money in the winter.

[Unit 6]

Practice

Page 62

W: Wegener's theory surprised a lot of people. Back in 1915, not many people could explain why tectonic plates moved. But most of the things that people thought were wrong with the preliminary theory were later contradicted. The theory was right all along. But it did need some amendments. There were two major changes that solved the problems with the theory. (*Practice A ends.*) The first had to do with how continents moved. What made them move? Well, scientists found the answer. Plates move because of heat. The Earth's core is very hot. As we know, heat rises. This heat pushes on the plates. It can move them in different directions. Now, some people also thought the crust was too thick for plates to move through. Actually, they were right— plates move *on top of* the crust. The hard part of the crust moves over a soft layer of the crust. This discovery solved the second problem.

Test

Page 64

M: Many theories try to state how the continents will move. Some think they will only move a little, and others say they will move a lot. But one theory is easier to believe than the others. The theory says that, just like in the past, we will one day have one huge continent again. They call this Pangaea Ultima. This will happen in two main ways. First, Africa will move *a lot*. Now, it is near what we call the middle of the Earth—the equator. However, it will move very far north. It will fill in the gap between North America and Europe. Those three will become one continent. In addition, South America will move northeast. First, it will hit the African plate. But it will also rotate. The long *tail* of the continent will then point east. It will actually meet with the south of Asia. So, once again, the Earth will be one big continent.

Transcript

[Review 1]

Integrated 1

Page 68

M: You'd be surprised how many plants in nature move. Many movements aren't visible to humans. That's because they happen so slowly. So it isn't likely that you'll see a nastic movement. But let me tell you about two plants that do move rather quickly. The first I want to talk about is the Venus Flytrap. You may have heard of this plant before. It is an example of hyponasty. It moves when it is touched. See, the Venus Flytrap eats insects. When an insect touches the inside of the plant, it closes. This is one of the most obvious nastic movements in nature. The second plant is called the Mimosa. This plant demonstrates thermonasty. The plant's leaves can fold up if the temperature changes. It does this to protect the leaves from harm. It's quite amazing to watch. In an experiment, I held a flame near a leaf of the Mimosa. The leaf began to fold up toward the center.

Integrated 2

Page 70

M: The legend of Atlantis is a popular story. Many people want it to be true. Some pretend there is evidence to support it being a real place. Really, there's nothing that says Atlantis was a real place. In fact, two things contradict the idea. First, there's nothing in the sea that says it ever existed. In fact, all the evidence says it was never there. Let me explain. The theory says an entire continent fell into the ocean. That means that parts of the crust of the continent would be on the ocean floor. But there isn't. All of the samples taken from that area have only found ocean crust. Thus, there's only ocean down there. There's no continent. Second, some people think that Bermuda and the Bahamas used to be parts of Atlantis. But there's no reason to think this. They're close to where people thought Atlantis was. Yet there's nothing to suggest they were part of a lost continent. We'd have to find the continent before we say that.

[Unit 7]

Practice

Page 78

M: The story in *Star Wars* shares quite a few things with myths. In what ways are they similar? Let's start with the characters. Luke Skywalker is the hero. He is very similar to other heroes in myths. (*Practice A ends.*) First, he uses *the force*. The force is a magical power that only some people can use. Magic is very common in myths. Only heroes can use magic wisely and fairly. Luke also later finds out that his parents were royalty. Most heroes grow up not knowing that they are special in some way. To continue, the story is also very similar to myths. Most myths start when a hero must leave home after a tragedy and go on a journey. *Star Wars* begins in the same way. Luke's home is attacked and he leaves on a long journey. The hero's motives are also often the same. The hero must always search for something. In *Star Wars*, the hero must search for his enemy, Darth Vader.

Test

Page 80

W: Have you heard of H.G. Wells? He wrote *The War of the Worlds* in 1898. It was a story about aliens from Mars attacking Earth in the future. However, the story was actually meant to comment on the world. It did this in two ways. First, it commented on events from Wells's time. In the story, aliens from Mars attack the Earth. The people on Earth have to defend themselves from the attack. They don't understand why the aliens are attacking. With this, Wells was commenting on real wars. He wanted people to see what it would be like if Earth were attacked for no reason. In addition, he was commenting on the future. Wells believed that life might exist on Mars. In his book, he explored this. He wrote about just one possibility of meeting life from another planet. He described how the world might react to aliens. Thus, he was commenting on both the present and the future.

[Unit 8]

Practice

Page 88

M: There are a lot of points against ethanol. Many people are quick to label it a failed idea. Notwithstanding those points, ethanol is still a good way to get rid of fossil fuels. Many of the cases against ethanol aren't correct. Let's look at two of the points against it. (*Practice A ends.*) To begin, some people say making ethanol uses too much energy. It uses more energy than it creates. Well, this used to be true—twenty-five years ago. It is easier to make ethanol today. So now ethanol actually creates *more* energy than it takes to make. Some people also say that we would need more land to make it than we have. This isn't true. We would have to make a lot of new farms to make ethanol. But scientists have come up with better ways to make ethanol. In the future, less corn will be needed to make the same amount of ethanol.

Test

Page 90

W: For some, wind power is an exciting new source of energy. Some even think it can replace fossil fuels. However, this is not the case. There are many problems with wind power, and these problems will prevent wind power from being a good way to replace fossil fuels. There are two main problems with wind power. First, it *does* pollute the world. Fossil fuels pollute the Earth with gases. Wind power, on the other hand, pollutes the Earth with noise. Wind power stations are very noisy places. The people who have to live by them say that it makes it almost impossible to sleep. Also, wind power is not truly sustainable. Some people live in very windy places. These places are great for wind power. But what about places where it isn't windy? Many places just don't have a lot of wind. And without wind, there is no wind power. When you think about these two things, it seems that wind power isn't so great after all.

[Unit 9]

Practice

Page 98

M: A new study tested the effects of sleep loss. The study tested people for a series of nights. For the three nights, they slept for eight hours. For the next six, they only got four hours of sleep. The study found two conclusions. (*Practice A ends.*) First, people didn't seem as alert or as smart when they got four hours of sleep. Their ability to use logic to solve problems wasn't very good. They even noticed that knowledge acquisition was affected. Why? Well, it seemed that the brain used most of its power to keep the person awake. To move on, sleep loss also affected the way the rest of the body works. It affected how the body produces insulin. Insulin is what the body uses to store sugars. But the body doesn't produce it correctly when someone gets fewer than eight hours of sleep. This makes people think that sleep loss might also cause diabetes.

Test

Page 100

W: People have studied sleep loss for a long time now. Still, we don't know everything that happens in the brain when you don't get enough sleep. Many studies have found interesting things about sleep loss. One study found two things about sleep loss in rats. First, the study found that rats can't find their way around when they don't sleep enough. It affects their ability to get where they want to go. They found that the rested rats could remember how to get through a maze. Rats that didn't sleep enough had trouble. They couldn't remember how to go through the maze. To continue, sleep loss also keeps the brain from recovering from use. The study looked at a certain part of the brain. When the rats didn't sleep, a part of the brain didn't work correctly. It couldn't make new brain cells in that area. Sleep is an important part of making new brain cells.

Transcript

[Unit 10]

Practice

Page 108

M: When a new computer comes out a month from now, how much faster do you think it will be? Can you predict that? People who believe in Moore's Law think you can. However, Moore's Law isn't a credible law—it's a mere guideline. It can, and will, change at some point in the future. There are two good reasons to believe this. (***Practice A ends.***) First, Moore's Law is true solely because people *want it to be true*. Computer makers do their best to follow Moore's Law, so it's not like Moore's Law just happens. If people didn't try to follow Moore's Law, it wouldn't be true. Secondly, the law has been true in the past, but it can't go on forever. At some point, it will stop. Someday, they won't be able to fit more transistors on a chip. And when this happens, the law won't be true anymore. Really, Moore's Law isn't a law at all.

Test

Page 110

W: The idea that computers can think is exciting and frightening at the same time. What will happen if computers learn to think without our help? Well, this isn't a problem we're likely to have. While AI is an interesting idea, it will never happen. Computers will never be able to *think*. Let me give you two reasons why this is true. First, computers really can't learn. Computers have to be programmed to learn. They can't learn anything that someone doesn't tell them to learn. So, really, it isn't *learning* at all. It's just really clever programming. OK, on to my next point. Computers will never be able to reason like humans can. Have you ever been presented with a unique problem? Did you find a way to solve it? Sure you did. Humans have a type of reasoning that a machine will never have. Machines can only solve problems that it knows how to solve. Therefore, machines will never be intelligent.

[Unit 11]

Practice

Page 118

W: The notion that Athenian democracy was good is something that a lot of people would reject. From my perspective, it was bad for the people. Let's look at two reasons why this is true. First, some think that all people voted in *all* laws. But there were certain clauses that made this untrue. If you lived close to the city walls, you couldn't vote in anything about war. (***Practice A ends.***) The government thought that people living there would always vote against wars. That's because other armies would always attack the walls, and people living there wouldn't want that. In addition, some people think it is good because you can vote on everything. Well, think about that for a moment. Is that really a good thing? Would you really want to vote on *everything*? Of course not. So it just meant people had to vote on useless stuff. It's better to have a government do all of that boring stuff for you.

Test

Page 120

M: Aristotle was a student of Plato. In many ways, they had very similar views. They agreed that the best rulers had to be good. But they didn't fully agree on what *good* was. Aristotle had a lot of different notions of good. From his perspective, two things made a person good. First, like Plato, Aristotle believed that philosophical knowledge was good. But Aristotle thought that knowledge had to be used properly. He said that knowledge had to be used to make people happy. Happiness was the greatest good for people. Second, Aristotle also thought a ruler should do good things. But he had a different idea of why rulers do them. For Aristotle, people did good things because they wanted to. Good things made them happy. But there weren't any people who were just good or bad. Anyone could start to do good things. So, in that way, he was different from Plato.

[Unit 12]

M: One animal study yielded some surprising results. A chimp named Washoe learned a human language in the 1980s. It wasn't a spoken language though. It was sign language. Let's see why the study supports that idea. (*Practice A ends.*) First, to learn a language, an animal has to be able to use words. It must use certain words without being told to say them. Well, Washoe did this. The scientists monitored her language use for many years. She ended up learning over 250 different signs. She knew what each sign meant and how to use it. In addition, Washoe learned how to put different signs together. She came up with her own names for different things. For example, she called her toilet "dirty good" and called a refrigerator "open food drink." No one taught her to say these things. But she learned how to do it all on her own.

W: Animals can learn language. Not many people would say that is false. Writing is a different story. Yet writing is not too difficult for animals. Kanzi is a bonobo, which is like a chimp, and he learned how to write. Let's look at the two ways he learned to write. First, he had to learn to understand language. To do this, Kanzi learned symbols called lexigrams. A lexigram is a very simple symbol. Kanzi could point to the lexigram that represented a certain object. For example, in the woods, Kanzi touched the symbol for fire on a piece of paper. So the researcher gave him wood and a lighter, and he made a fire. Thus, he knew what the symbol meant. Second, he learned how to write these symbols. At one point, he was looking outside. He wanted to go into the woods. Suddenly, he took a piece of chalk and wrote lexigrams for the woods. Thus, he knew how to write symbols, and he knew what they meant.

[Review 2]

Integrated 1

M: How does an author construct his or her story? Many authors look to their pasts to make a story. One such author was Mark Twain. One of his most famous books was *The Adventures of Tom Sawyer*, which was based on Mark Twain's childhood. Let's look at two ways he used his childhood in the book. First, he used characters from his childhood in the book. The main character is Tom Sawyer. Tom is actually based on Mark Twain as a child. The other characters are based on friends of Twain. Of course, the book is still fiction, but to make good characters Twain used real people. Twain also based the events of the book on real events. The book is about Twain's childhood growing up, and Twain even said that most of the events in the book really happened. In the book, Tom makes some friends paint a fence that he didn't want to paint. This was based on a real event in Twain's life.

Integrated 2

W: What is the point of the media? I mean, why do they exist? Whether it is a TV station or a newspaper, all media are businesses. As such, the aim of all media is to make money. In other words, the media don't serve the public interest. They just do whatever will make them the most money. Let me give you two reasons why this is true. To begin, TV networks show things that make them money. This is most evident from commercials. The only reason networks show commercials is to make money. Commercials don't really serve the public interest. Most people hate commercials, right? So it's all about what is good for business. Now, even the news that we hear is the same way. Most of the time, we don't get the news we need. We get entertaining news. That's because news stations and newspapers need to make money. So they need to draw in viewers. They do this by picking news that will keep people entertained, not informed.

Answer Key

[Unit 1]

Independent

Page 7

B
1. The best animal for a pet is <u>a dog</u>.
2. I like <u>that dogs are loyal and friendly</u>.
3. It is a good pet because <u>a dog will get along well with people and it is easy to care for</u>.
4. My family would <u>love to have a dog</u>.

Page 8

B
(A) Agree

C
Topic: Pets are <u>very important</u> members of the family.
A. A pet is <u>an important component of many families</u>.
  1. Many people attempt to <u>include their pets in their daily lives</u>.
  2. In my family, we like our dogs <u>to watch TV with us</u>.
B. Pets can give <u>sympathy to humans like a family member does</u>.
  1. Dogs are good at knowing <u>when a person is suffering or lonely</u>.
  2. When I am sad, my dogs <u>will try to cheer me up</u>.
  3. When I play with them, it <u>relieves me of my sadness</u>.
Conclusion: I think that <u>pets are very important family members</u>.

D
In fact,
The first is
For example
Second
Therefore

Page 9

E
(B) Disagree

F
Topic: Pets are <u>not the same</u> as other family members.
A. Pets do not contribute <u>anything to the family</u>.
  1. Family members should contribute by doing things like <u>washing dishes or cooking</u>.
  2. The only job of pets is to <u>eat, to sleep, and to play</u>.
B. Some people spoil their pets but are unfriendly <u>to their family members</u>.

1. It is sad not to care for your <u>relationships with your family</u>.
2. The whole family suffers when you <u>give pets too much importance</u>.
Conclusion: I think it is not good to treat pets <u>as importantly as other family members</u>.

G
First of all
Secondly
For these reasons

H
1. attempt   2. component   3. relieve
4. sympathy   5. suffer

Page 10

Sample Answer 1
Step 2

<u>agree</u>

Step 3

Topic: Pets are <u>just</u> as important as family members.
A. <u>Pets are just as important as people are because they bring a lot of happiness to families</u>.
  1. <u>In my family, our dog loves to play</u>.
  2. <u>Playing with my dog relieves my troubles</u>.
B. <u>Pets also help take care of their families</u>.
  1. <u>My dog barks when dangerous people are around</u>.
  2. <u>Our cat catches mice</u>.
Conclusion: <u>It is for these reasons that I think that pets are very important family members</u>.

Step 4

    I think that pets are <u>very important</u> members of a family. There are two reasons why <u>pets are such valuable components of a family</u>. First, I think this because <u>they bring a lot of happiness to families. Pets are good at cheering people up. For example, in my family, our dog loves to play. When I get to play with my dog, I feel relieved of all my troubles. Playing with him makes me happy.</u> Second, pets also <u>take care of their families</u>. For instance, <u>my dog attempts to protect our family at the first sign of danger. He will bark very loud if he knows that dangerous people are around. We also have a cat that likes to catch mice and rats. No family wants rats and mice around their house. So, our cat helps us too.</u> It is for these reasons that I think <u>pets are very important family members</u>.

Sample Answer 2
Step 2

disagree

Step 3

Topic: Pets are <u>not</u> as important as family members.
A. <u>First of all, pets cannot take care of themselves</u>.
    1. <u>In my family, everyone helps out, but not the pets</u>.
    2. <u>Pets need us to feed them</u>.
B. <u>Second, pets do not care about family the way people do</u>.
    1. <u>Pets are like children, but they never grow up</u>.
    2. <u>Our dog destroyed furniture and got into trouble</u>.
Conclusion: <u>It is for these reasons that I think that pets are not important family members</u>.

Step 4

    I think that pets are <u>not as important as other</u> members of a family. There are two reasons why <u>I think this</u>. First, I think this because <u>pets cannot take care of themselves. Everyone in the family helps each other, but pets need people. For example, they need us to feed them and to take them outside. We spoil them like young children. But unlike children, they never grow up</u>. Second, pets also <u>do not care about the family in the same way that people do</u>. For instance, <u>when we had a dog, he chewed on our furniture and destroyed it. My parents were angry, because they work very hard to buy us things. They were relieved when we got rid of the dog. Also, he got into a lot of trouble with the neighbors</u>. It is for these reasons that I think <u>pets are not as valuable as other family members are</u>.

Integrated

Page 11

B
1. (A)
2. They might talk about the reasons why Rome fell, and who and what caused it.

Page 12

A
(B)

B
Reading

Main idea: Rome fell because of its military.

Key points:
- Rome did not have a good <u>leader</u>.
- Not many people wanted to <u>join the Roman military</u>.

Lecture

Main idea: External military forces caused the fall of Rome.

Key points:
- The Persians captured <u>the Roman leader</u>, which hurt Rome's military.
  - Rome's troops were no longer as <u>sure of their military</u>.
  - It also <u>took a good leader away</u> from Rome.
- Barbarians attacked <u>Rome many times</u>.
  - This <u>weakened</u> Rome's infrastructure.
  - It also hurt <u>Rome's economy</u>.

Page 13

D
    The reading explains why Rome fell. The author says Rome fell because it had <u>a bad military</u>. There are two reasons why this is true.
    First, Rome did not have <u>good leaders</u>. One leader, Commodus, was especially bad. Even <u>the Roman troops</u> did not like him. This made the military weak.
    Second, the soldiers did not want to fight. Most people only fought because they <u>wanted money</u>. The army became weak because of this.
    The lecture, though, said that other militaries attacked Rome and caused it to fall. The Persians often attacked the Roman Empire. During one attack, they <u>captured the Roman leader</u>. This hurt Rome's confidence. In addition, barbarians attacked the empire.
    One group called the Goths often attacked. <u>The author says</u> they stole money and weakened Rome. These attacks caused Rome to fall.

E
1. infrastructure   2. external   3. decline
4. sustain   5. stability

Page 14

Step 1

Reading

Main idea: Rome fell because of problems with the economy.

Key points:
- The Goths began <u>to attack Rome and hurt the economy</u>.
  - Made it harder <u>to trade</u>
- Rome became <u>less wealthy</u>.
- The prices <u>in Rome went up</u>.

Answer Key

Lecture

Main idea: Rome's political troubles caused its fall.
Key points:
- Commodus became leader because <u>he was the son of the previous leader</u>.
  - This was a mistake because <u>he was not a good leader</u>.
  - He did not have much <u>political experience</u>.
- One of Rome's leaders <u>split the empire into two halves</u>.
  - This started a <u>civil war</u>.
  - It allowed the <u>barbarians to invade</u>.

Page 15
Step 3
Topic: The causes of the fall of Rome.
A. The reading says Rome fell because of <u>problems with the economy</u>.
  1. The Goths began <u>to attack Rome and hurt the economy</u>.
  2. The prices <u>of different things in Rome went up</u>.
B. The lecture says Rome's <u>political troubles</u> caused its fall.
  1. Commodus became leader because <u>he was the son of the previous leader</u>.
     - He was not <u>a good leader</u>.
     - He did not have much <u>political experience</u>.
  2. One of Rome's leaders <u>split the empire into two halves</u>.
     - Started a <u>civil war</u>
     - Allowed the <u>barbarians to invade</u>
Conclusion: The lecture and the reading differ because the reading states that <u>economic problems</u> caused the fall of Rome, and the lecture states that <u>political problems</u> caused it.

Step 4
The reading and the lecture discuss <u>what caused the fall of Rome</u>. The reading says that Rome fell because <u>of problems with the economy</u>. The reading says that <u>attacks from the Goths</u> made it harder to trade. The reading also says that <u>the prices of many things went up</u>.

The lecture says that Rome fell because <u>it had political troubles</u>. In the lecture, the speaker offers two points to support his theory. The first is that <u>Commodus became the leader of Rome because he was the son of the previous leader</u>. This was bad for two reasons. Commodus was <u>a bad leader, and he did not have much political experience</u>. The second point is that one of the leaders <u>of Rome split the empire</u>. This caused <u>a civil war that hurt the country</u>. It also allowed <u>the barbarians to invade</u>.

The reading and lecture differ because <u>the reading thinks economic problems caused the fall of Rome, while the lecture thinks political problems caused it</u>.

Check-up
Page 16
1. invades
2. valuable
3. troops
4. otherwise
5. cheer up
6. loyal
7. fall
8. spoil

[Unit 2]

Independent
Page 17
B
1. The experience was <u>when we went to the amusement park</u>.
2. We did this because <u>we like going on roller coasters</u>.
3. We <u>really enjoyed this experience</u>.
4. I think that <u>without money we could not have gone to the park</u>.

Page 18
B
(A) Agree

C
Topic: Borrowing money from a friend <u>is not</u> a good idea.
A. Asking to borrow money is <u>awkward</u>.
  1. It is even more awkward <u>between friends</u>.
  2. Asking for a loan from a friend <u>disrupts the relaxed nature of the friendship</u>.
  3. Makes it hard to <u>talk about other things</u>
B. Borrowing money becomes <u>a bigger problem if you can't pay it back</u>.
  1. To borrow money means <u>that you have to pay it back</u>.
  2. If you can't repay your friend, you <u>are going to feel guilty</u>.
  3. Feelings like that <u>can hinder communication between friends</u>.
Conclusion: If you want to retain your friendship, <u>don't borrow money from your friend</u>.

D
In fact
First
Second
However

E

(B) Disagree

F

Topic: It is <u>fine</u> to borrow money from a friend.
A. Friends should help each other <u>out with their problems</u>.
   1. I would never feel guilty <u>about asking my friend for money</u>.
   2. My friend knows <u>I would do the same for him</u>.
   3. In order to retain our friendship, <u>we must be there for each other</u>.
B. Helping out a friend with money problems <u>will not hinder a friendship</u>.
   1. It can make the friendship <u>stronger</u>.
   2. Friendship is about <u>trust</u>.
   3. Borrowing money can help build <u>trust between friends</u>.
Conclusion: In conclusion, borrowing money from a friend <u>is not a bad idea</u>.

G

Actually
First of all
For example
Secondly
Therefore
In conclusion

H

1. retain   2. disrupt   3. nature
4. hinder   5. guilty

Page 20

Sample Answer 1
Step 2

<u>disagree</u>

Step 3

Topic: Borrowing money from a friend <u>will not harm a friendship</u>.
A. <u>Borrowing money from a friend is better than borrowing money from a stranger</u>.
   1. <u>A friend knows you well and can be trusted</u>.
   2. <u>I wouldn't want to borrow money from someone I couldn't trust</u>.
B. <u>If someone is your friend, borrowing money shouldn't be a problem</u>.
   1. <u>A real friend would not feel bad about helping you</u>.
   2. <u>I wouldn't feel guilty if I had to ask my friend for a loan</u>.
Conclusion: <u>Therefore, I think that borrowing money from a friend is not a problem</u>.

Step 4

I think that <u>borrowing money from a friend will not harm a good friendship. There are two reasons why I think this is the case. First, it is better to take a loan from a friend than from a stranger</u>. For instance, <u>a friend knows you well and can be trusted. Asking for money will not disrupt that feeling of trust. However, you can't trust strangers</u>. Moreover, <u>I wouldn't want to borrow money from someone I couldn't trust</u>. Secondly, <u>if someone is your friend, then borrowing money from them shouldn't be a problem. The nature of friendship is to help each other</u>. For example, <u>a real friend will not feel bad about helping you with whatever you need. Similarly, I wouldn't feel guilty if I had to ask my friend for money. Good friends will not let things like money become a problem between them</u>. Therefore, I think that <u>borrowing money from a friend is not a problem</u>.

Sample Answer 2
Step 2

<u>agree</u>

Step 3

Topic: Borrowing money from a friend <u>will damage the friendship</u>.
A. <u>First, friends should help each other in other ways</u>.
   1. <u>For instance, lots of people in the world are not friendly to each other</u>.
   2. <u>Moreover, friends are the people to help you with their advice</u>.
B. <u>Secondly, money gets in the way of friendships</u>.
   1. <u>For example, my brother lost his best friend because he gave him a loan</u>.
   2. <u>Good friends usually refuse to borrow money from each other</u>.
Conclusion: <u>Therefore, I think that borrowing money from a friend is a bad idea</u>.

Step 4

I think that <u>borrowing money from a friend will damage the relationship. There are two reasons I feel this way. First, friends should help each other in other ways. For instance, lots of people in the world are not friendly to each other. However, a friend is someone you can ask for advice when you feel sad or have a problem you cannot solve. I wouldn't want to rely on strangers for help. Moreover, friends are the people to help you with their advice. Secondly, money only gets in the way of friendships. For example, my brother lost his best friend because he gave him a loan. The friend never repaid it and that was the end of their friendship. Good friends usually refuse to borrow money from each other</u>.

Answer Key

They don't want to cause something bad to happen to their friendship. Therefore, I think that borrowing money from a friend is a bad idea. It is the fastest way to hinder a good friendship.

Integrated

Page 21

B

1. (B)
2. They might talk about the ways that buildings change and why they have to change.

Page 22

A

(A)

B

Reading

Main idea: Building designs change when they are moved to another country.

Key points:
- Building in different climates can change a building's design.
- Many countries must use different materials.

Lecture

Main idea: Churches in New Mexico had to transform from Spanish designs.

Key points:
- Spain and New Mexico have different climates.
  - Spain's climate is mild, but New Mexico's can be very hot.
  - New Mexico churches were not built with large windows.
- The churches in New Mexico used different materials.
  - The Spanish churches were made of stone.
  - The builders in New Mexico didn't have stone, so they built with mud.

Page 23

D

The reading says that building designs must change when they are moved to a new country. The author offers two points to support this. First, a location's climate can make builders change a design. Other times, some builders have to alter a building's design because they have different materials to build with.

The lecture supports the reading by giving an example. The speaker discusses churches in New Mexico. The speaker says the designs came from Spain but changed. First, Spain and New Mexico have different climates. Spain is mild, but New Mexico is sometimes very hot. Therefore, the churches in New Mexico do not have large windows. The builders in New Mexico also had to use different materials. Spanish churches used stone, but the builders in New Mexico used mud.

E

1. thus
2. fundamental
3. alter
4. evolve
5. transform

Page 24

Step 1

Reading

Main idea: Many builders change designs from history to make them more modern.

Key points:
- They can change designs to use new materials.
- Some buildings can change designs to match the new style.

Lecture

Main idea: Old building designs transform when they are used for modern buildings.

Key points:
- Buildings change when new materials are made.
  - Older buildings did not use the strong metals we have today.
  - Many new buildings use steel.
- Some cultures have different styles.
  - Leaves were a popular symbol in Greece.
  - When Greek buildings are made today, symbols of corn are used.

Page 25

Step 3

Topic: The changes to buildings when they are built in different countries.

A. The reading says that builders change designs to make them more modern.
  1. Builders change designs to use new materials.
  2. Builders also change designs to match a more modern style.
B. The lecture supports the reading with examples.
  1. Buildings can change when new materials are made.
    - Buildings in the past did not use the strong materials we have today.
    - Many new buildings use steel.
  2. Buildings can change when cultures have different styles.

- Leaves were <u>a popular symbol used in Greece</u>.
- A modern building made in the Greek style used <u>symbols of corn</u>.

Conclusion: Designs can change when used in a <u>new place</u>.

Step 4

The reading and the lecture discuss <u>the ways that buildings change when they are built in a new country</u>. The reading says <u>many builders change building designs to make them more modern</u>. Builders <u>can change designs to use new materials</u>. Builders also <u>change designs to match the new country's styles</u>.

The lecture <u>supports the reading with examples</u>. First, the speaker says that buildings can change <u>when new materials are made. Buildings in the past did not use the strong materials that we have today</u>. Many new buildings <u>use strong materials like steel</u>. Second, the speaker says that buildings <u>can change when cultures have different styles</u>.

For example, leaves were <u>used as a popular symbol on many buildings in Greece</u>. A building built recently with a Greek style used <u>symbols of corn instead of leaves</u>.

In conclusion, the lecture confirms that designs <u>do change when they are used in a new place</u>.

Check-up

Page 26

1. materials
2. repay
3. loan
4. stranger
5. circulate
6. feelings
7. fairly
8. dirt

[Unit 3]

Independent

Page 27

B

1. That person is <u>my father</u>.
2. That person is well behaved because <u>he treats other people with respect</u>.
3. I feel <u>like I admire him and want to be the same as him</u>.
4. They act like <u>they respect him, too</u>.

Page 28

B

(A) Agree

C

Topic: Children today <u>do not behave</u> as well as children did in the past.

A. Kids today <u>are less polite than they were before</u>.
   1. In the past, <u>kids were more polite</u>.
   2. Almost every kid back then <u>was more modest in public</u>.
B. Kids no longer <u>have respect for their elders</u>.
   1. Many kids in school <u>don't listen to teachers</u>.
   2. They didn't do that as much in the past <u>as they do now</u>.
Conclusion: <u>I don't think kids today behave as well as children once did</u>.

D

The first is
The second thing
For example
Even worse
For these reasons

Page 29

E

(B) Disagree

F

Topic: Children today <u>do behave</u> as well as children in the past.

A. Children have <u>always been naughty</u>.
   1. My parents didn't listen <u>to the teacher</u>.
   2. They wrote <u>notes in class</u>.
B. Kids today don't behave <u>any worse than kids did before</u>.
   1. It is the nature of a child <u>to have fun and break the rules</u>.
   2. Playing with video games and cell phones <u>is not bad behavior</u>.
Conclusion: I think that children <u>do not behave any worse than kids did in the past</u>.

G

In my opinion
Sometimes
However
Obviously
Secondly
However
In conclusion

H

1. overall
2. obvious
3. criticism
4. modest
5. pretend

Answer Key

Page 30
Sample Answer 1
Step 2
agree

Step 3
Topic: Children today <u>do not behave</u> as well as children in the past.
A. <u>Children are less polite today.</u>
   1. <u>They don't say "please" and "thank you."</u>
   2. <u>They are not modest in public.</u>
B. <u>Children today don't respect their elders.</u>
   1. <u>They don't listen to their teachers.</u>
   2. <u>Some students pretend to be good but act badly when the teacher is not looking.</u>
Conclusion: This is why I think that children <u>today do not behave as well as children in the past</u>.

Step 4
   I think that <u>children today do not behave as well as children in the past</u>. I think this for two reasons. First, <u>children are less polite today. They used to be more polite in the past</u>. For example, <u>kids today don't say "please" and "thank you."</u> In my opinion, <u>they are not modest in public. Kids were not like this in the past</u>. Secondly, <u>children do not respect their elders. Today, children don't listen to their teachers</u>. For example, <u>sometimes children pretend to be good, but they act badly when the teacher is not there</u>. For these reasons, <u>I think that children today do not behave as well as children in the past</u>.

Sample Answer 2
Step 2
disagree

Step 3
Topic: Children today <u>do behave</u> as well as children in the past.
A. <u>Children have always been naughty</u>.
   1. <u>It is a child's nature to break the rules.</u>
   2. <u>My parents didn't listen to the teacher when they were in school.</u>
B. <u>Children are no worse than children in the past</u>.
   1. <u>They have more distractions today.</u>
   2. <u>Playing with video games and cell phones is not a bad thing.</u>
Conclusion: This is why I think that children <u>today behave as well as children in the past.</u>

Step 4
   I think that <u>children today behave as well as children in the past</u>. I think this for two reasons. First, <u>children have always been naughty. They are not</u>

<u>naughtier now than they were back then</u>. For example, <u>my parents didn't listen to their teacher when they were in school</u>. In my opinion, <u>it is a child's nature to break the rules</u>. Secondly, <u>children really are no worse now than they were in the past. Today, children have many more distractions than our parents did</u>. For example, <u>they play with video games and cell phones. I don't think this is a bad thing</u>. For these reasons, <u>I think that children today behave as well as children in the past</u>.

Integrated

Page 31
B
1. (B)
2. They might talk about the things that made botany popular and the people that affected its popularity.

Page 32
A
(B)

B
Reading
Main idea: Ordinary people made botany popular.
Key points:
• People <u>opened big gardens</u> where ordinary people could enjoy plants.
• Botany was <u>easy for all types of people to study</u>.

Lecture
Main idea: Botany became popular because of science.
Key points:
• The study of plants had <u>many medical uses</u>.
  - Plants were <u>used in cures</u>.
  - People wanted to see <u>how many could be used in medicine</u>.
• Lots of scientists wanted <u>to find every plant in the world</u>.
  - Many of them created <u>systems to catalog plants</u>.
  - The public also <u>wanted to join the search</u>.

Page 33
D
   The reading says that botany became popular because of <u>ordinary people</u>. The author supports this with two pieces of evidence. First, <u>the author says</u> people opened botanical gardens where ordinary people could go <u>to enjoy plants</u>. Also, botany was easy for ordinary people to study because it is not a complex science.

The lecture, however, says that botany became popular because of science. The speaker believes this for two reasons. First, botany was often used in medicine. Plants were sometimes used in cures. Because of that, ordinary people wanted to study botany too.

In addition, the speaker says that scientists wanted to make a list of all the plants in the world. Many of them created systems to catalog plants. After that, the public joined the hunt for new plants.

E

1. medical   2. facilitate   3. catalog
4. transition   5. comprehensive

Page 34

Step 1

Reading

Main idea: The public helped botany transform from a hobby to a science.
Key points:
• Botanical gardens were meant for the public.
• Botany was not done by scientists at first.

Lecture

Main idea: Botany became a science when scientists became interested in it.
Key points:
• Universities created their own botanical gardens where people could study botany.
  - Original botanical gardens were meant for the public.
  - University botanical gardens allowed scientists to study plants and learn that botany was important.
• Carl Linnaeus helped botany change from a hobby to a science.
  - He created a system to put plants into groups.
  - After that, people wanted to find plants and put them into groups.

Page 35

Step 3

Topic: The reasons why botany became a science.
A. The reading says that botany became a science because of the public.
  1. Botanical gardens were places that were meant for the public.
  2. At first, botany was not studied by scientists.
B. The lecture says that botany became a science when scientists began to study it.
  1. Universities created botanical gardens where scientists could study.

• Botanical gardens were originally meant for the public.
• University botanical gardens allowed scientists to study plants and learn that botany was important.
  2. Botany became more academic when Carl Linnaeus began to study plants.
    • Carl Linnaeus created a system that put plants into groups.
    • After that, people wanted to find new plants and put them into groups.
Conclusion: Therefore, scientists made botany a true science.

Step 4

The reading and the lecture discuss the reasons why botany became a science. The reading says that botany became a science because of the public. Botanical gardens were places that were meant for the public. At first, botany was not studied by scientists.

The lecture, however, disagrees. The lecture says that botany became a science when scientists began to study it. To begin, the speaker says that universities created their own botanical gardens. Botanical gardens were originally meant for the public. University botanical gardens allowed scientists to study plants and learn that botany was important. Second, the speaker says that botany became more academic when Carl Linnaeus began to study plants. Carl Linnaeus created a system that put plants into groups. After that, people wanted to find new plants and put them into groups.

In conclusion, the lecture disagrees with the reading because the reading believes that the public helped botany become academic, while the lecture says that scientists made it a true science.

Check-up

Page 36

1. illness   2. elders   3. public
4. polite   5. naughty   6. treat
7. cure   8. worse

[Unit 4]

Independent

Page 37

B
1. The activity was camping with my friends.
2. The group consisted of me and my three classmates.
3. I felt that it was a lot of fun and that I'd like to go again.

Answer Key

4. I participated in the group because <u>they are my best friends</u>.

Page 38
B
(B) Disagree

C
Topic: Belonging to a group or organization is <u>not important</u>.
A. Groups are mainly for people <u>who are not independent</u>.
  1. I don't agree that joining a group or team <u>makes you feel good</u>.
  2. I prefer to work alone and know <u>that my accomplishments are only mine</u>.
B. A lot of people join a group because <u>they don't want to be alone</u>.
  1. Being alone is <u>an important part of life</u>.
  2. I'd rather spend <u>most of my time alone</u>.
Conclusion: I think that <u>groups are not very important</u>.

D
For example
Secondly
However
Of course
Therefore

Page 39
E
(A) Agree

F
Topic: Being part of a group or organization <u>is very important</u>.
A. I think that many people <u>join a group to make friends</u>.
  1. I joined the soccer team in high school <u>in order to meet people</u>.
  2. I made <u>some great friends there</u>.
B. Being part of a group <u>allows us to achieve more than we can do on our own</u>.
  1. Soccer taught me <u>the value of teamwork</u>.
  2. On a team, everyone must assist each other <u>to score a goal and win</u>.
Conclusion: I think that groups, like a soccer team, <u>are an important part of life</u>.

G
To begin with
For example
For these reasons

H
1. Regardless   2. teamwork   3. assist
4. team   5. point of view

Page 40
Sample Answer 1
Step 2
<u>agree</u>

Step 3
Topic: Belonging to a group or organization <u>is a good idea</u>.
A. <u>People join groups to make friends.</u>
  1. <u>People are naturally social.</u>
  2. <u>Everyone, even an independent person, enjoys being part of a group.</u>
B. <u>Some think that groups help the people in them.</u>
  1. <u>The members of my church help each other when we have problems.</u>
  2. <u>When we work as a team, we feel stronger and can solve our problems.</u>
Conclusion: <u>I think that groups are a very important part of life.</u>

Step 4
I think that <u>belonging to a group or organization is a good idea</u>. First, <u>people join groups to make friends</u>. I say this because <u>people are naturally social. They enjoy being with other people. When you are young, you have your family. However, when you get older, you want to meet new people. Joining a group is a great way to do this. Everyone, even an independent person, enjoys being part of a group.</u> Secondly, <u>I feel that groups are important because they help the people in them. For example, the members of my church group help each other when we have problems. When we work as a team, we feel stronger and can solve our problems. It is that spirit of teamwork and sharing that makes groups so helpful to people. For these two reasons, I think that groups are a very important part of life.</u>

Sample Answer 2
Step 2
<u>disagree</u>

Step 3
Topic: Belonging to a group or organization <u>is not that important</u>.
A. <u>People can have interesting lives without joining a group</u>
  1. <u>People that don't belong to groups still do great things.</u>
  2. <u>Everyone says my cousin is a great singer, but she prefers singing alone. She doesn't like singing groups.</u>

B. Some think that groups show the "value of teamwork" as being very good; however, I don't agree with that point of view.
1. The members of my work group don't work well as a team.
2. When we work as a team, one person often does more work than the other people.
Conclusion: I don't think that groups are very important in life.

Step 4

I think that belonging to a group or organization is not that important. First, people can have interesting lives without joining groups. I say this because people that don't belong to groups still do great things. Look at Tiger Woods for example. He is not on a team, but he is famous around the world. Everyone says my cousin is a great singer, but she prefers to sing alone. She doesn't like singing groups. Secondly, some think that working in groups teaches the value of teamwork. I disagree. For example, the members of my work group don't work well as a team. When we work as a team, one person does more work than the other people. That is not fair. For these two reasons, I think that groups are not a very important part of life.

Integrated

Page 41

B

1. (A)
2. They might talk about how carbon dating works and why it is precise.

Page 42

A

(A)

B

Reading

Main idea: Carbon dating is a precise way to find the age of an artifact.

Key points:
• Carbon decays at a fixed rate.
• All plants and animals have the same fraction of carbon and carbon radiation.

Lecture

Main idea: Carbon dating is not a very precise process.
Key points:
• Carbon has not always decayed at the same rate.

- Carbon decayed much faster in the past.
- There's no way to know how long it used to take for carbon to decay.
• Carbon dating can only date things less than 40,000 years old.
- If it is older than that, there's too little carbon left.
- It is a technique that can't be used in all types of studies.

Page 43

D

The reading says that carbon dating is a precise way to find the age of artifacts. The author supports this with two points. First, carbon decays at a fixed rate. The author also says that all plants and animals have the same fraction of carbon and carbon radiation.

The lecture, on the other hand, says that carbon dating is not precise. The speaker gives two pieces of evidence to support this viewpoint. The speaker says that carbon has not always decayed at the same rate. Carbon decayed much more quickly in the past. There's no way we can know exactly how it decayed in the past. Also, carbon dating can only date objects that are less than 40,000 years old. If the object is older than that, there is not enough carbon left. Therefore, it is a technique that can't be used in all situations.

E

1. radiation   2. equation   3. definite
4. derive   5. identical

Page 44

Step 1

Reading

Main idea: There are two ways that carbon dating can be improved.
Key points:
• Scientists need to calibrate their results using tree rings.
• Scientists must remove harmful chemicals from items by using other chemicals.

Lecture

Main idea: The two possible solutions to carbon dating problems won't work.
Key points:
• Using tree rings to make dating more precise won't work.
- Not many trees have been around for long enough.
- One tree can only be used to date something in one place.

Answer Key

- Using chemicals makes dating <u>less precise</u>.
  - Some scientists use <u>chemicals to preserve items</u>.
  - These chemicals can <u>change the results of carbon dating</u>.

Page 45

Step 3

Topic: How carbon dating can be improved.
A. The reading says that there are <u>two ways that carbon dating can be improved</u>.
   1. Scientists need to <u>calibrate their results using tree rings</u>.
   2. Scientists must <u>remove harmful chemicals from items by using other chemicals</u>.
B. The lecture says that <u>the two possible solutions to carbon dating problems won't work</u>.
   1. Using tree rings <u>to make dating more precise won't work</u>.
      • Not many trees have <u>been around for long enough</u>.
      • One tree can only be used <u>to date something in one place</u>.
   2. Using chemicals makes <u>dating less precise</u>.
      • Some scientists <u>use chemicals to preserve items</u>.
      • These chemicals <u>can change the results of carbon dating</u>.
Conclusion: Therefore, these two ideas <u>cannot make carbon dating better</u>.

Step 4

The reading and the lecture discuss <u>whether the process of carbon dating can be improved</u>. The reading says <u>there are two things that can be done to make carbon dating better</u>. Scientists need <u>to calibrate the process of carbon dating by using tree rings</u>. In addition, they must <u>remove any chemicals from an item by using chemicals that won't harm the item</u>.

The lecture challenges what is said in the reading. The speaker says that <u>the two solutions to improve carbon dating will not work.</u> To begin, the speaker says that <u>using tree rings to make carbon dating more precise will not work</u>. Not many trees <u>have been around long enough to be used in dating</u>. Also, one tree can only be used <u>to date an item found in the same place</u>. Second, the speaker says that using chemicals <u>actually makes dating less effective</u>. Some scientists <u>use chemicals to preserve artifacts</u>. However, these chemicals <u>can change the results of carbon dating</u>.

In conclusion, the lecture challenges the reading because <u>the lecture says that the things suggested in the reading will not work</u>.

Page 46

1. flawed
2. artifact
3. value
4. decay
5. unite
6. spirit
7. accomplishment
8. fixed

[Unit 5]

Independent

Page 47

B
1. I took part in <u>a volunteer opportunity to plant trees in the park</u>.
2. I did it with <u>my friends and family</u>.
3. I did it because <u>I want to make my environment better</u>.
4. I think that <u>it was a really fun experience</u>.

Page 48

B
(A) Agree

C
Topic: It is important for <u>young people to help their communities</u>.
A. Volunteering teaches <u>young people responsibility</u>.
   1. When they work for their community, <u>they learn about its problems</u>.
   2. They also learn <u>how they can help solve a problem</u>.
B. Volunteering <u>engages young people</u> in their communities.
   1. When they work to help their community, <u>they meet people</u>.
   2. Knowing people in the community <u>helps a kid to better integrate into it</u>.
Conclusion: Young people must help out in their areas because the benefits <u>are relevant to everyone.</u>

D
First
However
Second
However
Furthermore

Page 49

E
(B) Disagree

F

Topic: Young people should not <u>have to spend time working to help their community</u>.

A. Young people will spend <u>the rest of their lives working</u>.
  1. When you are young, <u>it is the only time you have to play</u>.
  2. Their free time is theirs alone, and they should <u>use it to have fun while they are still young</u>.
B. Kids must <u>make money when they work</u>.
  1. Usually, when you work to help your community, <u>you do it as a volunteer</u>.
  2. You should always get a reward <u>when you fulfill your responsibilities</u>.
Conclusion: I think that young people should <u>not have to work to help their communities</u>.

G

The first one
Even then
Next
Usually
Similarly
For these reasons

H

1. regard	2. integrate	3. relevant
4. engage	5. fulfill	

Page 50

Sample Answer 1
Step 2
<u>agree</u>

Step 3
Topic: Young people <u>should</u> volunteer to help their communities.
A. <u>Volunteering teaches people responsibility</u>.
  1. <u>Young people need to learn responsibility</u>.
  2. <u>Responsibility will help them in school and at work later in life</u>.
B. <u>Volunteering gets young people involved in the community</u>.
  1. <u>They can get out and meet people</u>.
  2. <u>They make new friends or important connections</u>.
Conclusion: For these reasons, I think that young people <u>should volunteer to help their communities</u>.

Step 4
I think that <u>young people should volunteer to help their communities</u>. First, <u>volunteering teaches responsibility. Responsibility is a good thing</u>. Furthermore, <u>young people need to learn responsibility. It is an important quality and will help young people. It can help them at school. It will</u>

also help them later in life when they are working. Second, <u>volunteering gets young people involved in the community</u>. For example, <u>young people can get out and meet new people. This will be good for their social lives</u>. In addition, <u>they make good friends or important connections for later in life</u>. In conclusion, <u>I think young people should volunteer to help their communities</u>.

Sample Answer 2
Step 2
<u>disagree</u>

Step 3
Topic: Young people <u>should not</u> volunteer to help their communities.
A. <u>Adults spend their whole lives working</u>.
  1. <u>Young people should spend their youth having fun</u>.
  2. <u>They won't have time to have fun when they grow up</u>.
B. <u>People should be rewarded for their work</u>.
  1. <u>Young people are rewarded for their work in school with good grades</u>.
  2. <u>Their time is valuable too, so they should be paid for work outside of school</u>.
Conclusion: For these reasons, I think that young people <u>should not volunteer to help their communities</u>.

Step 4
I think that <u>young people should not volunteer to help their communities</u>. First, <u>adults spend their whole lives working. Young people will have lots of chances to work in the future</u>. Furthermore, <u>young people should spend their youth having fun. You only get one childhood. You should enjoy it. Once young people grow up, they will go to work. They will get married. They will not have much time to do fun things</u>. Second, <u>people should be rewarded for their work</u>. As they say, "time is money." For example, <u>young people get rewarded for hard work at school with good grades</u>. In addition, <u>a young person's time is valuable, too. A young person should be rewarded for work outside of school, just like an adult</u>. In conclusion, <u>I think young people should not volunteer to help their communities</u>.

Integrated

Page 51

B
1. (B)
2. They might talk about some of the problems of running a seasonal business and how to solve them.

Answer Key

Page 52

A

(A)

B

Reading

Main idea: Two things can help a seasonal business succeed.

Key points:
- A merchant must make a lot of money when it is open.
- Seasonal merchants have to plan ahead.

Lecture

Main idea: A theme park makes enough money to close in the winter.

Key points:
- Making money is the main objective.
  - The owners try not to spend too much money when the park is open.
  - They sell enough tickets to give them money for the winter.
- They have to plan ahead.
  - The park must pay to fix rides when they break.
  - The park also has to pay taxes even when it's closed.

Page 53

D

The reading says that seasonal businesses can be difficult to run. The author suggests two things that seasonal business owners can do. First, the business must generate a lot of revenue. In addition, the owners must plan ahead.

The lecture supports the reading by using a theme park as an example. The speaker discusses two things that the theme park does. First, the speaker says that making money is the main objective. The owners try not to spend too much money when the park is open. They also make a lot of money by selling tickets. In addition, the owners have to plan ahead. They sometimes have to pay to repair rides. They also have to pay taxes even when the park is closed.

E

1. generate   2. objective   3. merchant
4. revenue   5. adjustment

Page 54

Step 1

Reading

Main idea: Seasonal merchants must find ways to make money when business is slow.

Key points:
- Some business owners own more than one business.
- Business owners sometimes have to add new products to their stores.

Lecture

Main idea: Seasonal businesses can succeed by trying new things.

Key points:
- One seasonal business did well by opening a new store.
  - At first, the owner owned a landscaping business.
  - Because business was bad in the winter, she started a holiday supplies business.
- A second seasonal merchant succeeded by adding new products to the store.
  - The store sold outdoor furniture.
  - She began to sell other indoor products because business was bad in cold seasons.

Page 55

Step 3

Topic: How seasonal businesses can make money when business is slow.

A. There are two ways that a seasonal business can do this.
  1. To begin, some business owners have more than one kind of business.
  2. Also, business owners sometimes have to add new products to their stores.

B. The lecture says that seasonal businesses can succeed by trying new things.
  1. One seasonal business did well by opening a new store.
     - At first, the owner had a landscaping business.
     - Because business was bad in the winter, the business owner started a holiday supplies business.
  2. Another seasonal merchant succeeded by adding new products to the store.
     - The store sold outdoor furniture.
     - The owner began to sell other indoor products because business was bad in cold seasons.

Conclusion: The lecture supports the reading by giving examples of two successful businesses.

Step 4

The reading and the lecture discuss how seasonal businesses can make money when business is slow. The reading mentions two ways that seasonal business can do this. To begin, some business owners have more than one kind of business. Also, business owners sometimes have to add new products to their stores.

The lecture says that seasonal businesses can succeed by trying new things. One seasonal business did well by opening a new store. At first, the owner had a landscaping business. Because business was bad in the winter, the business owner started a holiday supplies business. Another seasonal merchant succeeded by adding new products to the store. The store sold outdoor furniture. The owner began to sell other indoor products because business was bad in cold seasons.

In conclusion, the lecture supports the reading by giving examples of two businesses.

Check-up

Page 56

1. rebel	2. theme park	3. Similarly
4. volunteer	5. control	6. free time
7. ride	8. run	

[Unit 6]

Independent

Page 57

B
1. I saw many different kinds of animals.
2. I went there because it was a school field trip.
3. I liked that I could learn about animals from all over the world.
4. I didn't like that some of the animals looked sad.

Page 58

B
(B) Disagree

C
Topic: Zoos are useful and very important.
A. Zoos protect threatened animals.
   1. Some animal populations cannot survive alone.
   2. Zoos give them a safe home.
B. Zoos teach people about nature.
   1. Zoos can teach people in cities about the importance of nature.
   2. They can teach people about respecting and protecting all the plants and animals on the Earth.
Conclusion: Zoos are useful because they save the lives of endangered animals and teach people to conserve nature.

D
In fact
First
Also
Mainly
However
In conclusion

Page 59

E
(A) Agree

F
Topic: Zoos are not useful.
A. Zoos are expensive.
   1. Caring for a large population of animals from around the world is expensive.
   2. It is less expensive to protect the domestic animals in our communities.
B. Zoos do not teach people to respect nature.
   1. They teach people not to respect nature.
   2. It is better to let animals be free and roam in nature.
Conclusion: Zoos are not useful, so we should eliminate them.

G
In fact
For example
Second
Actually
To conclude
Rather

H

1. population	2. domestic	3. decade
4. eliminate	5. conservation	

Page 60

Sample Answer 1
Step 2
agree

Step 3
Topic: Zoos are not very good and serve no useful purpose.
A. They take animals out of nature and lock them in cages.
   1. An animal should be free.
   2. Animals in zoos are not happy; they are sad.
B. Many people say zoos are for education, but I disagree.
   1. Zoos are mostly about entertainment.
   2. When we visited the zoo with our school, we didn't learn anything; we just had fun.
Conclusion: I don't think that zoos serve any useful purpose.

Step 4

I think <u>that zoos are not very good. They serve no useful purpose</u>. First, <u>they take animals out of nature and put them in cages</u>. I think <u>this is not right. I think animals should be free, not locked in a cage</u>. Also, <u>animals in a zoo are not very happy, they are sad. I think they are sad because they are not free</u>. Second, <u>many people say that zoos are for education, but I disagree. They are not for education</u>. I feel that <u>zoos are mostly for entertainment. They are there for fun and amusement</u>. In addition, <u>when we visited the zoo with our school, we didn't learn anything special. We just ran around and had fun</u>. In conclusion, <u>I don't think that zoos serve any useful purpose</u>.

Sample Answer 2
Step 2
<u>disagree</u>

Step 3

Topic: Zoos are <u>great and useful</u>.
A. <u>They are educational</u>.
  1. <u>They teach people about endangered animals</u>.
  2. <u>They teach children the importance of nature conservation</u>.
B. <u>Zoos provide healthy entertainment</u>.
  1. <u>Today, too many children spend time playing video games</u>.
  2. <u>When they visit the zoo, they can walk around and get exercise</u>.
Conclusion: <u>I think zoos serve a very useful purpose</u>.

Step 4

I think <u>that zoos are great and useful. They are also a lot of fun</u>. First, <u>they are educational. This is a good thing</u>. I think <u>that zoos teach people about endangered animals. This is a very important thing</u>. Also, <u>they teach children about the importance of nature conservation. This is also very important</u>. Second, <u>zoos provide healthy entertainment</u>. I feel that <u>too many children today waste time staying inside and playing video games. Going to the zoo will get them outside</u>. In addition, <u>when they visit the zoo, they can walk around and get some exercise</u>. In conclusion, <u>I think that zoos are great</u>.

Integrated

Page 61
B
1. (A)
2. They might talk about why the theory was wrong and what the correct theory is.

Page 62
A
(A)

B
Reading

Main idea: There were two problems with Wegener's theory of plate tectonics.
Key points:
• Wegener could not say <u>why the plates moved</u>.
• Many people did not think <u>it was possible for the plates to move through the crust</u>.

Lecture

Main idea: Two major changes solved the problems of Wegener's theory.
Key points:
• The first solved the problem of <u>why the plates move</u>.
  - Plates move because of <u>heat from inside the Earth</u>.
  - The heat from the Earth's core <u>pushes on the plates and makes them move</u>.
• People thought the crust was <u>too thick for plates to move through</u>.
  - Plates actually move <u>on top of the crust</u>.
  - The hard part of the crust <u>moves on top of a soft layer of crust</u>.

Page 63
D

The reading says that there were two problems with <u>Wegener's theory</u> of plate tectonics. <u>The author describes</u> the two problems. First, Wegener could not explain why the plates moved. In addition, many scientists did not think that plates could move through the thick crust.

The lecture differs from the reading because it explains how those problems were solved. The speaker says that two <u>major amendments</u> fixed the problems with Wegener's theory. First, scientists discovered <u>why the plates move</u>. Plates move because of heat from the Earth's core. Heat <u>pushes on</u> the plates and makes them move. Second, the author says that people thought that the crust was too thick for plates to move through. Plates actually move on top of <u>the crust</u>. The hard part of the crust moves on top of a soft part of the crust.

E
1. visible   2. amendment   3. complement
4. contradict   5. preliminary

Page 64

Step 1

Reading

Main idea: In the future, the continents will go through two major changes.

Key points:
- Asia and Africa <u>will join to make one continent</u>.
- North and South America <u>will move farther to the west</u>.

Lecture

Main idea: The continents will form another huge continent called Pangaea Ultima.

Key points:
- Africa will <u>move a great deal to the north</u>.
  - Africa will move from <u>the middle of the planet</u> to <u>the far north</u>.
  - It will <u>fill in the gap between North America and Europe</u> to make one continent.
- South America will <u>move to the northeast</u>.
  - The continent will hit <u>the African plate</u>.
  - The tail of the continent will <u>rotate to the east and join with Asia</u>.

Page 65

Step 3

Topic: How the continents will move in the future.

A. The reading says that they will <u>go through two major changes</u>.
   1. To begin, <u>Asia and Africa will join to make one continent</u>
   2. In addition, <u>North and South America will move farther to the west</u>.
B. The lecture, on the other hand, <u>says that the continents will form another huge continent called Pangaea Ultima</u>.
   1. First, Africa will <u>move a great deal to the north</u>.
      - It will move <u>from the middle of the planet to the far north</u>.
      - It will <u>fill in the gap between North America and Europe to make one continent</u>.
   2. Also, South America will <u>move to the northeast</u>.
      - The continent will <u>hit the African plate</u>.
      - The tail of the continent <u>will rotate to the east and join with Asia</u>.
Conclusion: The lecture says that <u>the continents will form one big continent</u> instead of <u>only having two major changes</u>.

Step 4

The reading and the lecture are about <u>how the continents will move in the future</u>. The reading says <u>that they will go through two major changes</u>. To begin, <u>Asia and Africa will join to make one continent</u>.

In addition, <u>North and South America will move farther to the west</u>.

The lecture, on the other hand, <u>says that the continents will form another huge continent called Pangaea Ultima</u>. First, Africa will <u>move a great deal to the north</u>. It will move <u>from the middle of the planet to the far north</u>. It will <u>fill in the gap between North America and Europe to make one continent</u>. Also, South America will <u>move to the northeast</u>. The continent will <u>hit the African plate</u>. The tail of the continent <u>will rotate to the east and join with Asia</u>.

In conclusion, the lecture disagrees with the reading because the lecture says <u>that the continents will form one big continent instead of only having two major changes</u>.

Check-up

Page 66

1. endangered
2. importance
3. discovery
4. plate
5. crust
6. threatened
7. roam
8. tectonic

[Review 1]

Independent 1

Page 67

Sample Answer 1
Step 2
<u>agree</u>

Step 3

Topic: American TV is <u>better than</u> Asian TV.
A. <u>The effects are much better.</u>
   1. <u>American TV has many more explosions and cool special effects.</u>
   2. <u>One TV show I like has really realistic looking robots.</u>
B. <u>There is more variety in American TV.</u>
   1. <u>I can always find something to watch on American TV.</u>
   2. <u>There are action shows, dramas, and even reality shows.</u>
Conclusion: This is why American TV <u>is better than Asian TV</u>.

Step 4

I think that American TV <u>is better than</u> Asian TV. I think this because <u>the effects on American TV are much better</u>. I think <u>American TV has many more explosions and cool special effects</u>. For example, <u>one TV show I like has really realistic looking robots</u>. Also, I think that <u>there is more variety in American TV</u>. I feel that <u>I can always find something</u>

Answer Key

to watch on American TV. I think this because <u>there are action shows, dramas, and even reality shows</u>. In conclusion, this is why American TV <u>is better than Asian TV</u>.

Sample Answer 2
Step 2
<u>disagree</u>

Step 3
Topic: American TV is <u>not better than</u> Asian TV.
A. <u>Asian TV is not as violent as American TV.</u>
  1. <u>Soap operas are not about people dying all the time.</u>
  2. <u>One of my favorite Korean soap operas is about a historical doctor.</u>
B. <u>The stories on Asian TV are better than American TV.</u>
  1. <u>The plots are more natural than on American TV.</u>
  2. <u>Korean soap operas have really good plot development.</u>
Conclusion: This is why American TV <u>is not as good as Asian TV</u>.

Step 4
   I think that American TV <u>is not better than</u> Asian TV. I think this because <u>Asian TV is not as violent as American TV</u>. I think <u>Korean soap operas are not about people dying all the time</u>. For example, <u>one of my favorite Korean soap operas is about a historical doctor</u>. Also, I think that <u>the stories on Asian TV are better than American TV</u>. I feel that <u>the plots are more natural than on American TV</u>. I think this because <u>Korean soap operas have really good plot development.</u> In conclusion, this is why American TV <u>is not as good as Asian TV</u>.

Integrated 1
Page 68
Step 1
Reading
Main idea: A nastic movement happens when <u>an external force disrupts a plant and causes it to move.</u>
Key points:
- Hyponasty occurs when a plant moves because <u>it is touched by something</u>.
- Thermonasty happens because of <u>changes in temperature around the plant</u>.

Lecture
Main idea: There are two plants that <u>demonstrate nastic movements</u>.

Key points:
- One plant that uses nastic movement is called the <u>Venus Flytrap</u>.
  - It is an example of <u>a plant that uses hyponasty, which is a response to touch</u>.
  - The plant closes when an insect <u>touches the inside of the plant</u>.
- Another plant that demonstrates nastic movement is the <u>Mimosa</u>.
  - This plant uses a movement called <u>thermonasty, which is a response to temperature</u>.
  - The plant's leaves can <u>fold up</u> if the temperature changes.

Page 69
Step 3
Topic: The reading and the lecture discuss nastic movements in plants.
A. The reading discusses two types of <u>nastic movements</u> and says how they happen.
  1. The first type is called <u>hyponasty</u>, and it happens when <u>a plant responds to touch</u>.
  2. The second type is called <u>thermonasty</u>, which is <u>when a plant responds to temperature changes</u>.
B. The lecture <u>supports the reading</u> by discussing two examples of nastic movements in nature.
  1. The <u>Venus Flytrap</u> is a plant that uses nastic movements.
   • Its movement is a type <u>called hyponasty, or a movement in response to touch</u>.
   • The plant closes when <u>an insect touches the inside of the plant</u>.
  2. Another type of plant that uses nastic movements is called the <u>Mimosa</u>.
   • The plant uses a kind of movement called <u>thermonasty, or a response to temperature changes</u>.
   • If the temperature around the plant changes, its leaves <u>will fold up toward the middle</u>.
Conclusion: Therefore, the lecture <u>supports</u> the reading by <u>offering two examples of plants that use nastic movements</u>.

Step 4
   The reading and the lecture both discuss <u>nastic movements in plants</u>. The reading begins by discussing <u>two types of nastic movements and how they happen</u>. The first type mentioned is called <u>hyponasty</u>, and it happens when <u>a plant responds to touch</u>. The second type the author mentions is <u>thermonasty</u>, which <u>happens when a plant responds to temperature changes</u>.
   The lecture <u>supports the reading</u> by discussing <u>two examples of nastic movements in nature</u>. The speaker discusses the <u>Venus Flytrap</u>, a plant that

uses nastic movements. This plant's movement is an example of hyponasty because it moves in response to being touched. The plant closes when an insect touches the inside of the plant. The speaker also discusses a plant called the Mimosa. This plant uses a type of nastic movement called thermonasty, which is a response to temperature changes. If the temperature around the plant changes, its leaves will fold up toward the middle.

In conclusion, the lecture supports the reading by offering two examples of plants that use nastic movements.

Integrated 2

Page 70

Step 1

Reading

Main idea: There is proof that the lost continent of Atlantis existed.

Key points:
- Some evidence of Atlantis has been found at the bottom of the ocean.
- The remains of Atlantis can also be seen above the water.

Lecture

Main idea: There is nothing to suggest that Atlantis used to be a real place.

Key points:
- There's no evidence at the bottom of the sea that suggests Atlantis existed.
  - If a continent fell into the ocean, there would be continental crust in the ocean.
  - However, scientists have only found the regular crust of the ocean.
- There's no reason to think that Bermuda and the Bahamas used to be part of Atlantis.
  - There's nothing to suggest that they were ever part of a lost continent.
  - We would have to find the actual continent of Atlantis before we could say that.

Page 71

Step 3

Topic: The reading and the lecture discuss whether a place called Atlantis ever existed.

A. The reading suggests that Atlantis was a real continent in the past.
   1. Some evidence of Atlantis has been found at the bottom of the ocean.
   2. The remains of Atlantis can also be seen above the water.
B. The lecture refutes the information in the reading with two points.

1. There's no evidence at the bottom of the sea that suggests that Atlantis existed.
   - If a continent fell into the ocean, there would be continental crust in the ocean.
   - However, scientists have only found oceanic crust.
2. There's no reason to think that Bermuda and the Bahamas used to be part of Atlantis.
   - No evidence suggests that those places were part of a continent.
   - For this to be true, we would have to find the actual continent of Atlantis.

Conclusion: The lecture disagrees with the theories proposed in the reading.

Step 4

The reading and the lecture discuss whether a place called Atlantis ever existed. The reading begins by suggesting that Atlantis was a real continent in the past. First, the author says that some evidence of Atlantis has been found at the bottom of the ocean. In addition, the author says that the remains of Atlantis can also be seen above the water.

The lecture refutes the information in the reading by stating that there's no evidence that Atlantis was ever a real place. The speaker first says that there's no evidence of Atlantis at the bottom of the ocean. He says that if a continent fell into the ocean, then there would be continental crust in the ocean. However, scientists have only found the regular crust of the ocean. The speaker also says that there's no reason to think that Bermuda and the Bahamas used to be part of Atlantis. No evidence suggests that those places were part of a continent. For this to be true, we would have to find the actual continent of Atlantis.

In conclusion, the lecture disagrees with the theories proposed in the reading.

Independent 2

Page 72

Step 2

Sample Answer 1

agree

Step 3

Topic: Parents should not let their children play outside without an adult.

A. Playing outside can be dangerous.
   1. It is easy to get hurt playing outside.
   2. My friend tripped and fell and broke his finger.
B. Parents should keep an eye on what their kids are doing.
   1. Children can run into a lot of bad things when playing outside.

2. There is a bully in my neighborhood that likes to be mean to kids.

Conclusion: For these reasons, I think that parents should stay with their children when they play outside.

Step 4

I think that parents should not let their children play outside without an adult. To begin, I think playing outside can be dangerous. I think this because it is easy to get hurt playing outside. For example, my friend tripped and fell and broke his finger. Secondly, I believe parents should keep an eye on what their kids are doing. This is because children can run into a lot of bad things when playing outside. For example, there is a bully in my neighborhood that likes to be mean to kids. For these reasons, I think parents should stay with their children when they play outside.

Sample Answer 2
Step 2
disagree

Step 3

Topic: Parents should let their children play outside without an adult.
A. Kids need to learn how to play alone and be responsible.
   1. The only way for kids to grow up is to be given freedom.
   2. I am more responsible outside because my parents let me play outside alone.
B. Parents should encourage kids to play outside all the time.
   1. Parents shouldn't make their kids stay inside when they are busy.
   2. My parents are often busy inside, and I don't want to be stuck inside because they can't go outside to watch me.
Conclusion: For these reasons, I think that parents should let their children play outside without supervision.

Step 4

I think that parents should let their children play outside without an adult. To begin, I think kids need to learn how to play alone and be responsible. I think this because the only way for kids to grow up is to be given freedom. For example, I am more responsible outside because my parents let me play outside alone. Secondly, I believe parents should encourage kids to play outside all the time. This is because parents shouldn't make their kids stay inside when they are busy. For example, my parents

are often busy inside, and I don't want to be stuck inside because they can't go outside to watch me. For these reasons, I think parents should let their children play outside without supervision.

[Unit 7]

Independent

Page 73

B
1. The experience was when I was visiting my aunt and uncle.
2. I felt bad around the smoke.
3. I left the room when they smoked to get away from the smoke.
4. I think that it is bad for everyone.

Page 74

B
(A) Agree

C
Topic: Smoking should be banned in public.
A. Smoking is not only bad for the smoker, but it also harms other people.
   1. Smoking causes cancer in smokers and non-smokers alike.
   2. Second-hand smoke deprives non-smokers of clean, healthy air.
B. Smoking in public places sets a bad example for children.
   1. What children see around them influences their behavior.
   2. They can learn good habits or bad habits, like smoking.
Conclusion: It is a good idea to ban smoking in public places to protect the health of non-smokers and to set a good example for children.

D
First
Second
Clearly
Therefore

Page 75

E
(B) Disagree

F

Topic: Smoking <u>should not be</u> banned in public.

A. People have <u>the right to smoke</u>.
  1. They <u>have the freedom to</u> do things that harm them.
  2. Banning smoking deprives people <u>of their freedom to smoke</u>.
B. If non-smokers don't like smoke, <u>they can go to other public places</u>.
  1. Don't go to a nightclub if <u>you don't like being around smoke</u>.
  2. Non-smokers can <u>choose whether to go to places with smoking or not</u>.
Conclusion: It is not necessary t<u>o ban smoking from public places</u>.

G

First
However
Therefore
Second
For instance
In conclusion

H

1. favor   2. statistics   3. alike
4. deprived   5. mainstream

Page 76

Sample Answer 1
Step 2
<u>agree</u>

Step 3
Topic: I <u>think that</u> smoking should be banned in public places.
A. <u>Smoking smells bad and pollutes the air</u>.
  1. <u>It makes non-smokers uncomfortable</u>.
  2. <u>Second-hand smoke makes it difficult for non-smokers to enjoy their meals</u>.
B. <u>It will help people to smoke less</u>.
  1. <u>It will make smoking look bad</u>.
  2. <u>It will reduce the opportunities for people to smoke</u>.
Conclusion: I think <u>smoking should be banned in public places</u>.

Step 4
    In my opinion, <u>smoking should be banned in all public places</u>. I think this <u>for two reasons</u>. First, <u>smoking smells bad and pollutes the air. It is dirty and unhealthy. This is very bad</u>. Furthermore, <u>it makes non-smokers uncomfortable. They should be able to enjoy their lives, too. Also, second-hand smoke makes it difficult for people, especially non-smokers, to enjoy their meals</u>. Second, <u>banning smoking in</u>

<u>public places will help people smoke less. Also, it will make smoking look bad. This will help to make smoking unpopular. In addition, it will reduce the opportunities people have to smoke. This might help them slow down and quit</u>. Therefore, <u>I think that smoking should be banned in public places</u>.

Sample Answer 2
Step 2
<u>disagree</u>

Step 3
Topic: I <u>don't think that</u> smoking should be banned in public places.
A. <u>Banning smoking will cause people to smoke more in private</u>.
  1. <u>The result will be more harm to smokers and perhaps their families</u>.
  2. <u>It will still not get rid of second-hand smoke</u>.
B. <u>You can get rid of second-hand smoke with good air filters</u>.
  1. <u>The filters will clean pollution from the air</u>.
  2. <u>Banning smoking only gets rid of one kind of pollution</u>.
Conclusion: I think <u>smoking should not be banned in public places</u>.

Step 4
    In my opinion, <u>smoking should not be banned in all public places</u>. I think this <u>for two reasons</u>. First, <u>banning smoking will cause people to smoke more in private. This is bad for them</u>. Furthermore, <u>it will not only be bad for the smokers, it could be bad for their families as well. Also, banning smoking will not get rid of second-hand smoke</u>. Second, <u>you can get rid of second-hand smoke more effectively with good air filters</u>. Also, <u>these filters will remove smoke and other kinds of pollution from the air</u>. In addition, <u>banning smoking only removes one kind of pollution from the air</u>. Therefore, <u>I think that smoking should not be banned in public places</u>.

Integrated

Page 77

B
1. (A)
2. They might talk about what science fiction and myths have in common and what stories have these things in common.

Page 78

A
(B)

Answer Key

B

Reading

Main idea: Science fiction and myths have many things in common.

Key points:
- The characters in science fiction are similar to the ones in myths.
- The plots of science fiction and myths are similar.

Lecture

Main idea: *Star Wars* is similar in many ways to ancient myths.

Key points:
- The hero of *Star Wars* is very similar to heroes from ancient myths.
  - He can use a magical power called the force.
  - He also finds out he is a member of a royal family.
- The story of *Star Wars* is also similar to myths.
  - The hero's journey begins when his home is attacked.
  - The hero's motives are also often the same.

Page 79

D

The reading says that science fiction and myths are often very similar. The author supports this with two points. First, the characters in science fiction and myths can be very similar. In addition, the author states that the plots of science fiction and myths are often similar.

The lecture supports the reading using the example of *Star Wars*. The speaker first discusses the characters in *Star Wars* using the hero, Luke, as an example. The speaker says that Luke can use a magical power like many heroes in myths. In addition, he finds out in the story that he is royalty, which often happens to the heroes in myths. Second, the author says that *Star Wars* has a plot similar to myths. First, the hero's journey begins when his home is destroyed. In addition, the motives of the hero are similar to other heroes in myths.

E

1. plot   2. motive   3. legend
4. tragedy   5. evident

Page 80

Step 1

Reading

Main idea: Some writers use science fiction to comment on the world.

Key points:
- Some authors comment on the world by imagining the world in the future.
- Authors also write science fiction to comment on what the world might be like in the future.

Lecture

Main idea: *The War of the Worlds* was a story that was meant to comment on the world.

Key points:
- It commented on events from the time that Wells lived.
  - In the story, aliens from Mars attack Earth.
  - Wells was commenting on real wars.
- He was also commenting on the future.
  - Wells believed that life might exist on Mars.
  - He described how the people on Earth might react to aliens.

Page 81

Step 3

Topic: Science fiction can be a way for authors to offer social commentary.

A. The reading says that authors use science fiction to comment on the world.
  1. First, some authors comment on the world by imagining the world in the future.
  2. Also, authors write science fiction to comment on what the world might be like in the future.

B. The lecture supports the reading by using *War of the Worlds* as an example of a science fiction story that was meant to comment on the world.
  1. It commented on events from the time that Wells lived.
     - In the story, aliens from Mars attack Earth.
     - With this, Wells was commenting on real wars.
  2. He was also commenting on the future.
     - Wells believed that life might exist on Mars.
     - He described how the people on Earth might react to aliens.

Conclusion: Wells's story supports the reading because it uses science fiction to comment on the world in the present and in the future.

Step 4

The reading and the lecture say that science fiction can be a way for authors to offer social commentary. The reading says authors use science fiction to comment on the world. First, some authors comment on the world by imagining the world in the future. Also, authors write science fiction to comment on what the world might be like in the future.

The lecture supports the reading by using *War of the Worlds* as an example of a science fiction story that was meant to comment on the world. It commented on events from the time that Wells lived. In the story, aliens from Mars attack Earth. With this, Wells was commenting on real wars. He was also commenting on the future. Wells believed that life might exist on Mars. He described how the people on Earth might react to aliens.

In conclusion, Wells's story supports the reading because it uses science fiction to comment on the world in the present and in the future.

Check-up

Page 82

1. royalty
2. lungs
3. myth
4. Cancer
5. second-hand smoke
6. quest
7. non-smokers
8. hero

[Unit 8]

Independent

Page 83

B
1. My community is a city neighborhood near the university.
2. My school is very close to where I live.
3. It takes me about fifteen minutes if there is no traffic.
4. I like that we have good neighbors and lots of shops.

Page 84

B
(A) Agree

C
Topic: It is better to live close to where you work.
A. Living close to work saves time and money.
   1. If you live close to work, you can get there faster.
   2. If you live close to your job, you'll spend less money on gas.
B. Another benefit of living close to work is that you are less tired at the end of the day.
   1. Driving can make you tired.
   2. If you live close to work, you'll have more free time to relax.
Conclusion: I think it is better to live close to where you work.

D
For example
In fact
For these reasons

Page 85

E
(B) Disagree

F
Topic: It isn't good to live close to where you work.
A. I need to have distance between my work life and my personal life.
   1. I like to keep them separate, and a long commute helps me do that.
   2. It also helps me maximize the separation between my work life and my personal life.
B. I want a career in finance, which means I will work for a company located downtown.
   1. I don't want to live downtown since I prefer the suburbs.
   2. I would rather live some distance away from where I work.
Conclusion: I think that it's actually better not to live close to where you work.

G
First
For instance
Similarly
Second
However
Therefore
To sum up

H
1. maximize
2. fatigue
3. To sum up
4. downtown
5. exhausted

Page 86

Sample Answer 1
Step 2
agree

Step 3
Topic: It is better to live close to where you work.
A. When you live close to work, you won't have a long commute.
   1. A shorter drive means you will be less tired and more alert at work.
   2. You will have more free time to spend with friends and family.
B. If you live close to work, you will save money.
   1. A shorter drive means you will spend less on gas.
   2. A shorter drive means less damage and repairs to your car.
Conclusion: It is better to live close to work.

Step 4

I think that <u>it is better to live close to where you work</u>. First, <u>when you live close to work, you won't have a long commute. It is better to have a short drive to work</u>. For instance, <u>a shorter drive means you will be less tired. You'll be able to work harder at work and do more things when you get home</u>. In addition, <u>you'll have more time to spend with your family and friends. This is good for your health, too</u>. Second, <u>if you live closer to work, you will be able to save money</u>. For example, <u>you won't have to spend as much money on gas. Gas is getting expensive these days</u>. Also, <u>a shorter drive means less wear on your car. This means that your car will not break down so much. You will spend less on repairs</u>. To sum up, <u>I think it is better to live close to work</u>.

Sample Answer 2
Step 2
<u>disagree</u>

Step 3

Topic: <u>It is better to live far from where you work</u>.
A. <u>Most workplaces are in areas I wouldn't want to live</u>.
  1. <u>Most workplaces are in the city, but the city is too crowded</u>.
  2. <u>Living next to a factory could be noisy and dirty</u>.
B. <u>It is healthy to live far from where you work</u>.
  1. <u>It is healthy for you to separate your work life from your home life</u>.
  2. <u>The areas outside the city are often cleaner and healthier</u>.
Conclusion: <u>It is better to live far away from where you work</u>.

Step 4

I think that <u>it is better to live far from where you work</u>. First, <u>most workplaces are in areas I wouldn't want to live</u>. For instance, <u>most workplaces are in the city. The city is much too crowded for me</u>. In addition, <u>living next to a factory would be noisy and dirty</u>. Second, <u>it is healthy for you to live far from where you work</u>. For example, <u>it is good to separate your work life from your home life. This will reduce stress. This is good for you</u>. Also, <u>the areas outside the city are usually cleaner and healthier</u>. To sum up, <u>I think it is better to live far away from work</u>.

Integrated

Page 87
B
1. (B)

2. <u>They might talk about why ethanol can't replace gasoline or a different type of fuel that is better than ethanol</u>.

Page 88
A
(B)

B
Reading

Main idea: The problems with ethanol negate its benefits.

Key points:
- It takes more <u>energy</u> to make ethanol than <u>ethanol can produce</u>.
- Too much <u>land</u> is needed to grow the corn needed for ethanol.

Lecture

Main idea: The points against ethanol are not correct.
Key points:
- Some people say making ethanol uses <u>too much energy</u>.
  - It is easier to <u>make ethanol today</u>.
  - Ethanol now creates <u>more energy than is needed to make it</u>.
- Others say we would need <u>too much land to make ethanol</u>.
  - Scientists have come up with <u>better ways to make ethanol</u>.
  - In the future, less <u>corn will be needed to make ethanol</u>.

Page 89
D

The reading says that there are many problems with using ethanol as fuel, and these problems negate <u>its benefits</u>. The author uses two points to support this. First, ethanol <u>does not produce</u> as much energy as is needed to make it. In addition, too much land is needed to grow the corn needed for ethanol.

<u>The lecture disagrees</u> with the points made in the reading. The speaker mentions that some people think ethanol does not make enough energy. However, it is easier <u>to make</u> ethanol today. Ethanol now creates more energy than is needed to make it. In addition, the speaker says that <u>some people think</u> that too much land is needed to make ethanol. However, scientists have come up with new ways to make ethanol. In the future, less corn <u>will be needed</u> to make the same amount of ethanol.

E
1. label   2. substitute   3. Notwithstanding
4. negate   5. sustainable

Page 90

Step 1

Reading

Main idea: Wind power should be used as a replacement for fossil fuels.
Key points:
• Wind power does not <u>pollute the environment</u>.
• Wind power is <u>sustainable</u>.

Lecture

Main idea: There are two major problems with wind power.
Key points:
• Wind power does <u>pollute the Earth</u>.
  - Fossil fuels <u>pollute the Earth with harmful gases</u>.
  - Wind power <u>instead pollutes the Earth with noise</u>.
• Wind power is not <u>really sustainable</u>.
  - Some places do not have <u>very much wind</u>.
  - Without wind, <u>there can be no wind power</u>.

Page 91

Step 3

Topic: Whether wind power should be used as a replacement for fossil fuels.
A. The reading says that wind power <u>should be used as a replacement for fossil fuels</u>.
  1. Wind power does not <u>pollute the environment</u>.
  2. Wind power is <u>sustainable</u>.
B. The lecture says that there are <u>two major problems with wind power</u>.
  1. Wind power does <u>pollute the Earth</u>.
    • Fossil fuels <u>pollute the Earth with harmful gases</u>.
    • Wind power <u>instead pollutes the Earth with noise</u>.
  2. Wind power is not <u>really sustainable</u>.
    • Some places <u>do not have very much wind</u>.
    • Without wind, <u>there can be no wind power</u>.
Conclusion: Wind power is <u>not as great as some people say it is</u>.

Step 4

The reading and the lecture discuss <u>whether wind power should be used as a replacement for fossil fuels</u>. The reading says <u>wind power should be used as a replacement for fossil fuels</u>. To begin, wind power does not <u>pollute the environment</u>. Additionally, wind power is <u>sustainable</u>.

The lecture <u>says that there are two major problems with wind power</u>. First, wind power does <u>pollute the Earth</u>. Fossil fuels <u>pollute the Earth with harmful gases</u>. Wind power <u>instead pollutes the Earth with noise</u>. Second, the speaker says that wind power is not <u>really sustainable</u>. Some places <u>do not have very much wind</u>. Without wind, <u>there can be no wind power</u>.

In conclusion, the lecture says that <u>wind power is not as great as some people say it is</u>.

Check-up

Page 92

1. refinement   2. ethanol   3. suburbs
4. refine   5. commute   6. traffic
7. fossil fuel   8. distance

[Unit 9]

Independent

Page 93

B
1. I use the Internet <u>to search for information on studying English</u>.
2. They use the Internet <u>to watch funny movies and play video games</u>.
3. I have <u>sometimes used the Internet to help with my homework</u>.
4. They don't like the Internet because <u>they don't know how to use it</u>.

Page 94

B
(A) Agree

C
Topic: The Internet <u>does not give</u> reliable information.
A. Anyone can write whatever they want and <u>put it on the Internet</u>.
  1. When you read a newspaper or book, <u>you can trust the information</u>.
  2. That is not the case <u>with the Internet</u>.
B. On the Internet, people don't document where <u>their information comes from</u>.
  1. On the Internet, many people don't know <u>the source of the reports they read</u>.
  2. In journalism, you must tell where you get your information from so that it is <u>reliable</u> and readers <u>can trust you</u>.
Conclusion: The Internet is <u>not a good</u> source of reliable information.

Answer Key

D
First
However
Second
However
To sum up

Page 95

E
(B) Disagree

F
Topic: I think the Internet <u>gives</u> reliable information.
A. The Internet is democratic because it allows anyone with a computer <u>to share information</u>.
   1. This is a good thing because it makes it easier for people to <u>talk with each other</u>.
   2. If someone says something that is not true, <u>someone else will correct them</u>.
B. You can get excellent information about <u>products on the Internet</u>.
   1. This can help you make good decisions when <u>you want to buy something</u>.
   2. When I needed a new bike, I used the Internet to <u>get the bike I wanted</u>.
Conclusion: You <u>can find lots of</u> reliable information on the Internet.

G
First
Second
For example
In summary

H
1. document   2. reliable   3. assert
4. profession   5. journalism

Page 96

Sample Answer 1
Step 2
<u>agree</u>

Step 3
Topic: The Internet <u>does not give</u> reliable information.
A. <u>The Internet makes it easier for people to lie</u>.
   1. <u>Anyone can publish whatever they want on the Internet</u>.
   2. <u>It is difficult for us to know if the information is true or not</u>.
B. <u>The Internet does not state its sources</u>.
   1. <u>You don't know where the information comes from, so you can't trust it</u>.

   2. <u>You can trust newspapers and magazines because they state their sources</u>.
Conclusion: The Internet is <u>not a source</u> of reliable information.

Step 4
   I think that <u>the Internet does not give us very useful information</u>. I think this for two reasons. First, <u>the Internet makes it easier for people to lie</u>. For example, <u>anyone can publish anything they want on the Internet. Some people write things that are not true on purpose</u>. In addition, <u>it is very difficult for us to know if the information is true or not. Sometimes we might read something that is a lie, but we would think it is true. This is not good</u>. Second, <u>the Internet does not state its sources</u>. This means <u>that we don't know where the information we read comes from. Because of this, we can't trust it</u>. However, <u>I know I can trust newspapers or magazines. They must state their sources</u>. In summary, <u>the Internet is not a source of reliable information</u>.

Sample Answer 2
Step 2
<u>disagree</u>

Step 3
Topic: The Internet <u>gives</u> reliable information.
A. <u>The Internet is helpful for doing our school work</u>.
   1. <u>Anyone can use the Internet to help with homework</u>.
   2. <u>It is important to know how to find information</u>.
B. <u>The Internet can help you learn about subjects you don't study in school</u>.
   1. <u>You can learn about anything you want</u>.
   2. <u>Without the Internet, this would be very difficult</u>.
Conclusion: The Internet is <u>a source</u> of reliable information.

Step 4
   I think that <u>the Internet gives us very useful information</u>. I think this for two reasons. First, <u>the Internet is helpful for doing our school work</u>. For example, <u>anyone can use the Internet to help with their homework</u>. In addition, <u>it is important to know how to find information. This is an important skill to know in school and at work</u>. Second, <u>the Internet can help you learn about subjects that you don't study in school</u>. This means <u>that you can learn about anything you want. Not just the things the teacher tells you to study</u>. However, <u>without the Internet, this would be very difficult.</u> In summary, <u>the Internet is a source of reliable information</u>.

Integrated

Page 97

B

1. (A)
2. They might talk about how sleep affects the mind and what happens in the brain when someone doesn't get enough sleep.

Page 98

A

(A)

B

Reading

Main idea: Sleep loss can have many negative effects on the mind.

Key points:
- Sleep loss can change the way <u>the mind works</u>.
- Sleep loss also changes how <u>the body works</u>.

Lecture

Main idea: A study on sleep loss found two conclusions.

Key points:
- People didn't seem <u>as alert or smart when they didn't get enough sleep</u>.
  - Their ability to use <u>logic to solve problems</u> wasn't very good.
  - Even the <u>ability to learn</u> was affected.
- Sleep loss also affects the way <u>the body</u> works.
  - It affects how the body produces <u>insulin</u>.
  - The body doesn't <u>produce it correctly</u> when someone doesn't get enough sleep.

Page 99

D

The reading says that <u>sleep loss</u> can have many effects on the mind and body. <u>The author offers</u> two points to support this. To begin, the author says that sleep loss can affect how the mind works. In addition, it can make the body work incorrectly.

The lecture <u>supports the reading</u> with a study. The speaker begins by describing the study. The study found two conclusions. First, the study found that people didn't seem <u>as alert or smart</u> when they didn't get enough sleep. Their ability to use logic to solve problems wasn't very good. In addition, the way they learned was also affected. Second, the speaker says that sleep loss affects the way the body works. It changes the way the body <u>produces insulin</u>. The body is unable to <u>make it</u> correctly when a person doesn't get enough sleep.

E

1. regulate   2. psychological   3. mentally
4. acquisition   5. logic

Page 100

Step 1

Reading

Main idea: Lack of sleep can make it difficult for the brain to learn new things.

Key points:
- Sleep loss can make it harder to <u>learn simple things</u>.
- Sleep loss makes the brain unable to <u>rest</u>.

Lecture

Main idea: A study of sleep loss in rats found two things.

Key points:
- Rats can't <u>find their way around</u> when they don't get enough sleep.
  - Rested rats could easily remember <u>how to get through a maze</u>.
  - Rats that didn't sleep couldn't remember <u>how to get through it</u>.
- Sleep loss keeps the brain from <u>recovering from use</u>.
  - When the rats didn't sleep, a part of the brain <u>didn't work right</u>.
  - It couldn't make <u>new brain cells</u> in that area.

Page 101

Step 3

Topic: The effects of lack of sleep on the brain.

A. The reading says that lack of sleep can make it difficult for the brain <u>to learn new things</u>.
  1. Sleep loss can make it harder to <u>learn simple things</u>.
  2. Sleep loss makes the brain unable to <u>rest</u>.
B. The lecture describes a <u>study of sleep loss in rats</u>.
  1. Rats can't <u>find their way around when they don't get enough sleep</u>.
    • Rested rats could easily <u>remember how to get through a maze</u>.
    • Rats that didn't sleep <u>couldn't remember how to get through it</u>.
  2. Sleep loss keeps the brain from <u>recovering from use</u>.
    • When the rats didn't sleep, <u>a part of the brain didn't work right</u>.
    • It couldn't make <u>new brain cells in that area</u>.
Conclusion: Sleep loss keeps the brain from <u>working like it should</u>.

Answer Key

Step 4

The reading and the lecture discuss <u>the effects of lack of sleep on the brain</u>. The reading says that lack of sleep <u>can make it difficult for the brain to learn new things</u>. First, sleep loss can make it <u>harder to learn simple things</u>. Also, sleep loss makes the brain <u>unable to rest</u>.

The lecture describes a <u>study of sleep loss in rats</u>. First, the speaker says that rats can't <u>find their way around when they don't get enough sleep</u>. Rested rats could easily <u>remember how to get through a maze</u>. Rats that didn't sleep <u>couldn't remember how to get through it</u>. Second, the speaker says sleep loss keeps the brain from <u>recovering from use</u>. When the rats didn't sleep, <u>a part of the brain didn't work right</u>. It couldn't make new brain cells in that area.

In conclusion, the lecture supports the reading by <u>describing a study that confirms the points made in the reading</u>.

Check-up

Page 102

1. hormone
2. diabetes
3. accept
4. democratic
5. editor
6. chronic
7. insulin
8. reports

[Unit 10]

Independent

Page 103

B

1. The experience was <u>when I graduated from high school</u>.
2. I received the money from <u>my grandmother and my aunts and uncles</u>.
3. They gave me money <u>as a reward for getting good grades and graduating</u>.
4. I <u>spent it on clothing and some CDs</u>.

Page 104

B

(B) Disagree

C

Topic: Rich people <u>should not</u> give money to the poor.
A. Rich people work hard and deserve to <u>keep all the money they earn</u>.
   1. It is not proper <u>to take their money</u>.
   2. Some people work <u>harder than other people do</u>.

B. Giving money to poor people will <u>make them lazy</u>.
   1. If poor people want more money, they <u>will have to work for it</u>.
   2. That is how a market economy <u>works</u>.
Conclusion: Rich people <u>should not</u> give money to poor people.

D

First
Therefore
Moreover
Second
In conclusion

Page 105

E

(A) Agree

F

Topic: Rich people <u>should</u> give money to the poor.
A. Most rich people have more <u>money than they need</u>.
   1. They should give some of their money away to <u>help people who have less</u>.
   2. Many people do not have their basic needs met, such as <u>housing, food, or clothes</u>.
B. Rich people have a responsibility to <u>the society that gave them their riches</u>.
   1. Not everyone can <u>become rich</u>.
   2. Rich people, therefore, should use their money to <u>help other people enjoy things</u>.
Conclusion: I think the rich <u>should</u> give money to the poor.

G

First
For this reason
Secondly
For the above reasons

H

1. wealth
2. proportion
3. compensation
4. role
5. proper

Page 106

Sample Answer 1
Step 2
<u>disagree</u>

Step 3
Topic: Rich people <u>should not</u> give money to the poor.
A. <u>I think it is the government's role to help the poor</u>.
   1. <u>Rich people should not be responsible for that</u>.
   2. <u>If poor people need food or homes, the government will help them</u>.

B. Underline People receive fair compensation for their work.
  1. Rich people should be able to keep what they earn.
  2. When people can keep the money they earn, they will be motivated to earn more money.
Conclusion: I think that rich people should not give money to the poor.

Step 4

I think that rich people should not give their money to the poor. It is not right. I think this for two reasons. First, I think that it is the government's role to help the poor. I think that rich people should not be responsible for that. It is not their job. Also, if poor people need food or homes, the government can help them. Secondly, people receive fair compensation for their work. This means that rich people should keep what they earn. They worked for it. It is theirs. In addition, when people get to keep all the money they earn, they will be motivated to earn more money. It is for these reasons that I think rich people should not give money to the poor.

Sample Answer 2
Step 2
agree

Step 3
Topic: Rich people should give money to the poor.
A. It is proper for rich people to be leaders.
  1. Rich people should lead in improving society.
  2. If they give away their money, it will help others.
B. Rich people who do not give money to the poor are stingy and mean.
  1. Rich people should not do that because they set a bad example for everyone.
  2. When they are not generous, they will make enemies.
Conclusion: I think that rich people should give their money to the poor.

Step 4

I think that rich people should give their money to the poor. It is the right thing to do. I think this for two reasons. First, I think that it is proper for rich people to be leaders. I think rich people should lead in improving society. They have the money and knowledge to do so. Also, if they give money away, it will help others. Secondly, rich people who do not give money to the poor are stingy and mean. This means that rich people should not do that. If they do that, they will set a bad example for everyone else. In addition, when they are not generous, they will make enemies. It is for these reasons that I think rich people should give money to the poor.

Integrated

Page 107
B
1. (B)
2. They might talk about why Moore's Law is true and why it will not stop.

Page 108
A
(B)

B
Reading
Main idea: The theory of Moore's Law can be supported with two facts.

Key points:
- Moore's Law has been true in the past.
- Moore's Law will be true for many years in the future.

Lecture
Main idea: Moore's Law will not be true at some point in the future.

Key points:
- Moore's Law is only true because people want it to be true.
  - Computer makers try to follow Moore's Law.
  - It wouldn't be true if computer makers did not make it true.
- It has been true in the past, but it can't continue forever.
  - Someday, computer makers won't be able to put more transistors on a chip.
  - When this happens, Moore's Law will not be true anymore.

Page 109
D

The reading describes Moore's Law and gives reasons why it is true. The author says that it can be supported with two facts. First, Moore's Law has been true in the past. In addition, Moore's Law will continue for many years in the future.

The lecture disagrees with the reading. The speaker gives two reasons to support the idea that Moore's Law is not a real law. First, Moore's Law is only true because people want it to be true. Computer makers try to follow Moore's Law. If they didn't do this, the law would not be true. In addition, it has been true in the past, but it can't go on forever. Someday, computer makers won't be able to fit more transistors on a chip. When this happens, Moore's Law will no longer be true.

Answer Key

E
1. capacity   2. mere   3. credible
4. guidelines   5. solely

Page 110
Step 1
Reading

Main idea: We will someday have artificially intelligent computers.
Key points:
- Computers can now <u>learn on their own</u>.
- Some computers now know how to <u>reason like humans do</u>.

Lecture

Main idea: Computers will never be able to think.
Key points:
- Computers are not able to <u>learn</u>.
  - The only reason computers can learn is because <u>they are programmed to learn</u>.
  - It isn't learning; it is just <u>really good programming</u>.
- Computers will never be able to <u>reason in the way humans can</u>.
  - Humans have <u>a type of reasoning</u> that machines will never have.
  - Machines can only solve problems that <u>they know how to solve</u>.

Page 111
Step 3
Topic: Whether computers will ever be able to think.
A. We will someday have <u>artificially intelligent computers</u>.
    1. Computers can now <u>learn on their own</u>.
    2. Some computers now know <u>how to reason like humans do</u>.
B. The lecture says computers <u>will never be able to think</u>.
    1. Computers are not able to <u>learn</u>.
      • The only reason computers can learn is <u>because they are programmed to learn</u>.
      • It isn't learning; it is <u>just really good programming</u>.
    2. Computers will never be able to <u>reason in the way that humans can</u>.
      • Humans have <u>a type of reasoning that machines will never have</u>.
      • Machines can only solve problems that <u>they know how to solve</u>.
Conclusion: Therefore, machines <u>will never be able to think like humans do</u>.

Step 4

The reading and the lecture discuss <u>whether computers will ever be able to think</u>. The reading says <u>we will someday have artificially intelligent computers</u>. Computers can now <u>learn on their own</u>. Also, some computers now know <u>how to reason like humans do</u>.

The lecture says computers <u>will never be able to think</u>. First, computers are not able to <u>learn</u>. The only reason computers can learn is <u>because they are programmed to learn</u>. It isn't learning; it is <u>just really good programming</u>. Second, computers will never be able to <u>reason in the way that humans can</u>. Humans have <u>a type of reasoning that machines will never have</u>. Machines can only solve problems that <u>they know how to solve</u>.

In conclusion, the lecture disagrees with the reading because it says <u>machines will never be able to think like humans do</u>.

Check-up

Page 112
1. Someday   2. Stingy   3. expected
4. philanthropy   5. transistors   6. market economy
7. trend   8. Generous

[Unit 11]

Independent

Page 113
B
1. This person is <u>George Washington</u>.
2. This person was <u>the first president of the United States</u>.
3. They learn about <u>him</u> because <u>he is very important to our country's history</u>.
4. I would ask <u>him what he thinks of my country today</u>.

Page 114
B
(A) Agree

C
Topic: Learning about the past has <u>no value</u> for those living today.
A. The world today is <u>very different</u> than it was in the past.
    1. Learning about how people lived <u>in the past is useless</u>.
    2. Today, circumstances are so <u>different from those in the past</u>.

B. Learning about the past <u>wastes our time</u>.
  1. Learning about other subjects would help me <u>prepare for college</u>.
  2. Taking a computer class would also help me <u>get a better job in the future</u>.
Conclusion: I don't think there is any point to <u>learning about the past</u>.

D
First
Thus
Secondly
For example
In conclusion

Page 115

E
(B) Disagree

F
Topic: Learning about the past has <u>a lot of value</u> for those living today.
A. Our traditions remind us <u>of who we are</u>.
  1. They contain the wisdom of former generations; therefore, <u>they give us a framework for how to live our lives</u>.
  2. If we throw away our traditions, <u>we will forget where we come from</u>.
B. Learning about the past can help us <u>make decisions</u>.
  1. It can also help us avoid <u>making the same mistakes again</u>.
  2. We can study <u>these mistakes</u>.
Conclusion: I think it is <u>very valuable</u> for people today to learn about the past.

G
Therefore
Second
For example
For these reasons

H
1. framework   2. generation   3. former
4. circumstance   5. contribution

Page 116

Sample Answer 1
Step 2
<u>agree</u>

Step 3
Topic: Learning about the past <u>has no</u> value for those living today.

A. <u>Learning about history wastes my time</u>.
  1. <u>If I study history, then I am not paying attention to the present</u>.
  2. <u>It is better to prepare for the future</u>.
B. <u>History is boring</u>.
  1. <u>You will not learn anything when you study history</u>.
  2. <u>Things are more interesting today than in the past</u>.
Conclusion: I think that it is <u>not valuable</u> for people today to learn about the past.

Step 4
I think that <u>learning about the past has no value for those living today. None at all</u>. First, <u>learning history wastes my time. I am busy, so I don't have time to waste</u>. For example, <u>if I study history, then I am not paying any attention to the present. The present is what is important</u>. Also, <u>it is much better to prepare for the future. I can't change history, but I can change the future</u>. Secondly, <u>history is boring</u>. For example, <u>you won't learn anything when you study history. Who wants to spend time studying but not learning anything</u>? In addition, <u>things are more interesting today than in the past. They didn't really do anything interesting in the old days. These days, new technology makes the world more exciting</u>. In conclusion, <u>I think that it is not valuable for people today to learn about the past</u>.

Sample Answer 2
Step 2
disagree

Step 3
Topic: Learning about the past <u>has</u> value for those living today.
A. <u>Learning about the past helps us understand the present</u>.
  1. <u>If I study history, then I can understand the causes of global warming</u>.
  2. <u>As a result, I will be better prepared to do what I can to solve this problem</u>.
B. <u>Learning about the past gives us a framework for knowing our culture</u>.
  1. <u>You need to know about your history to understand your culture</u>.
  2. <u>Today this is very important</u>.
Conclusion: I think that it is <u>valuable</u> for people today to learn about the past.

Step 4
I think that <u>learning about the past has value for those living today</u>. First, <u>learning about the past helps us to understand the present</u>. For example, <u>if I study history, then I can understand the causes of</u>

Answer Key

today's problems. Also, <u>it will make me better prepared to deal with those problems</u>. Secondly, <u>learning about the past gives a framework for understanding our own culture</u>. For example, <u>you need to know your history before you can understand your culture</u>. In addition, <u>knowing about your own culture is very important today. The Internet is making the world a smaller place; so we should try to protect our culture</u>. In conclusion, <u>I think that it is valuable for people today to learn about the past</u>.

Integrated

Page 117

B

1. (A)
2. They might talk about how Athenian democracy worked and why it was good for Greece.

Page 118

A

(B)

B

Reading

Main idea: Athenian democracy was good for the government and the people.

Key points:
• It let all adults have <u>a voice in the government</u>.
• People were able to <u>vote on everything</u>.

Lecture

Main idea: Athenian democracy was bad for the people of Greece.
Key points:
• Not all people <u>were able to vote</u>.
  - There were certain <u>clauses</u> that made people unable to vote.
  - If you lived near the city walls, you couldn't <u>vote on wars</u>.
• It is not a good thing to have people vote <u>on everything</u>.
  - It meant that people have to vote on <u>useless laws</u>.
  - It is better to have <u>the government</u> handle small laws.

Page 119

D

The reading says that <u>Athenian democracy</u> was good for the people of Greece. The author gives two reasons for believing this. First, it let all adults

have <u>a voice</u> in the government. In addition, people were able to vote on everything.

<u>The lecture says</u> that this was not good for the people. First, not all people were <u>allowed to vote</u> on all of the laws. There were certain clauses that made some people unable to vote. For example, people who lived close to <u>the city walls</u> couldn't vote on things having to do with war. Second, it isn't a good thing to have people vote on everything. It meant that people had to vote even on <u>useless things</u>. It is better to have the government do that for the people.

E

1. clause   2. reject   3. perspective
4. mutually   5. notion

Page 120

Step 1

Reading

Main idea: Plato believed the best ruler was a philosopher-king.
Key points:
• Only philosopher-kings <u>truly understand the world</u>.
• Plato believed that good came from <u>doing good things for people</u>.

Lecture

Main idea: Plato and Aristotle agreed that rulers must be good, but disagreed on <u>how rulers became good</u>.
Key points:
• Like Plato, Aristotle thought <u>knowledge</u> was good.
  - Aristotle thought that it needed to be <u>used properly</u>.
  - Knowledge should be used to <u>make people happy</u>.
• Aristotle also thought a good ruler should <u>do good things for people</u>.
  - For Aristotle, people did good things because <u>it made them happy</u>.
  - There weren't any people that were <u>simply good or bad</u>.

Page 121

Step 3

Topic: The best type of ruler according to Plato and Aristotle.

A. The reading says that the best ruler is a <u>philosopher-king</u>.
  1. Only philosopher-kings <u>truly understand the world</u>.
  2. Plato believed that good came from <u>doing good things for people</u>.

B. The lecture says that Plato and Aristotle agreed that <u>rulers must be good</u>, but disagreed on <u>how rulers became good</u>.
  1. Like Plato, Aristotle thought <u>knowledge was good</u>.
     • He thought that it needed to be <u>used properly</u>.
     • Knowledge should be used to <u>make people happy</u>.
  2. Also like Plato, Aristotle thought <u>a good ruler should do good things</u>.
     • For Aristotle, people did good things because <u>it made them happy</u>.
     • There weren't any people that were <u>simply good or bad</u>.
Conclusion: In that way, Aristotle was <u>different</u> from Plato.

Step 4

The reading and the lecture discuss <u>Plato's and Aristotle's views on the best type of ruler</u>. The reading says <u>the best ruler is a philosopher-king</u>. Only philosopher-kings <u>truly understand the world</u>. Plato believed that good came from <u>doing good things for people</u>.

The lecture says that Plato and Aristotle <u>agreed that rulers must be good, but disagreed on how rulers became good</u>. Like Plato, Aristotle thought <u>knowledge was good</u>. He thought that it needed to be <u>used properly</u>. Knowledge should be used to <u>make people happy</u>. Second, Aristotle, like Plato, thought <u>a good ruler should do good things</u>. For Aristotle, people did good things because <u>it made them happy</u>. In addition, there weren't any people that were <u>simply good or bad</u>.

In conclusion, the lecture says that Plato and Aristotle <u>had different views</u>.

Check-up

Page 122

1. point
2. value
3. power
4. voice
5. useless
6. college
7. plenty
8. represent

[Unit 12]

Independent

Page 123

B
1. I visited <u>New York City</u>.
2. I visited that city because <u>my parents were taking me to see my aunt</u>.
3. I liked <u>the big buildings, the subway, and the park</u>.
4. I saw <u>both historic and modern buildings all over the city</u>.

Page 124

B
(A) Agree

C
Topic: Cities should <u>fix their old and historic buildings</u>.
A. Old buildings give a city <u>its character</u>.
  1. They make the city unique and tell <u>you about its history</u>.
  2. Many people visit cities just to <u>see the old buildings</u>.
B. Old buildings are usually better <u>built than new ones</u>.
  1. Many new buildings <u>are poor quality</u>.
  2. People made old <u>buildings better</u>.
Conclusion: It is better to <u>repair historic buildings</u> than replace them with <u>new ones</u>.

D
First
On the contrary
Second
In fact
For example
However
Clearly
Therefore

Page 125

E
(B) Disagree

F
Topic: Cities should <u>replace their old buildings with new ones</u>.
A. It is too expensive to <u>maintain old buildings</u>.
  1. Old buildings are a <u>constant problem to maintain</u>.
  2. New buildings are constructed using better technology, so they will have <u>fewer problems than old buildings</u>.
B. New buildings <u>look better</u>.
  1. They fit with <u>modern styles</u> and show <u>people the city is not stuck in the past</u>.
  2. Replacing old buildings is a good way to <u>improve a city's image</u>.
Conclusion: I think that all cities should replace their old buildings with new ones.

G
On the other hand
Therefore
Similarly
Second
Conversely
In conclusion
In fact

Answer Key

H
1. maintain   2. unrelated   3. conversely
4. construct   5. constant

Page 126
Sample Answer 1
Step 2
agree

Step 3
Topic: Cities should repair their old buildings.
A. Old buildings give a city its charms.
   1. Buildings are one of the most important features of a city.
   2. That is why people want to go there.
B. It is less disruptive to repair old buildings than to construct new ones.
   1. It is actually quite easy to maintain an old building.
   2. Tearing down old buildings is loud and also makes a big mess.
Conclusion: That's why I think that cities should repair their old buildings.

Step 4
    I think that cities should repair their old buildings. First, it is these old buildings that give a city its charms. New buildings are boring. Old buildings have character. For example, buildings are one of the most important features of a city. Furthermore, these buildings are why people want to go to visit these cities. Second, it is less disruptive to repair old buildings than to build new ones. For example, it is actually very easy to maintain an old building. It doesn't really take much work. Conversely, tearing down old buildings is loud and makes a big mess. Putting up a new building takes a long time. That's why I think that cities should repair their old buildings.

Sample Answer 2
Step 2
disagree

Step 3
Topic: Cities should not repair their old buildings.
A. Old buildings are difficult to maintain.
   1. Old buildings were built with old technology.
   2. These are hard to repair.
B. Old buildings do not fit with how we live today.
   1. Many old apartment buildings were built before people had cars.
   2. New apartment buildings can be built with parking spaces underground.
Conclusion: That's why I think that cities should not repair their old buildings.

Step 4
    I think that cities should not repair their old buildings. First, old buildings are difficult to maintain. It is not worth the time or the expense. For example, old buildings were built with old technology. They can't function very well in the modern world. Furthermore, these buildings are hard to repair. Why repair an old building when you can build a new one? Second, old buildings do not fit in with how we live today. Life today is much different than in the past. For example, many old buildings were built before people had cars. Parking was not a problem. Conversely, new apartment buildings can be built with parking spaces underground. This is much more convenient. That's why I think that cities should not repair their old buildings.

Integrated

Page 127
B
1. (A)
2. They might talk about whether animals can learn language and how they learn language, and give examples.

Page 128
A
(B)

B
Reading
Main idea: Animals must do two things in order to learn language.

Key points:
- An animal must be able to use words in some way.
- Animals must also combine words to form new thoughts.

Lecture
Main idea: A study of a chimp named Washoe proved that animals are able to learn language.

Key points:
- To learn language, an animal must be able to use words.
   - It must use certain words without being told to do so.
   - Washoe learned how to use over 250 different signs.

- Washoe learned how to put <u>signs together to make new thoughts</u>.
  - She came up with her own <u>names for different things</u>.
  - She learned how to say these things <u>all on her own</u>.

Page 129

D

The reading says that animals can <u>learn language</u> if they can do two things. First, an animal must be able to use words in some way. <u>In addition</u>, it must be able to combine words to form new thoughts.

The lecture <u>supports the reading</u> by describing a study in which a chimp named Washoe learned sign language. <u>The speaker describes</u> two things that Washoe did that support the idea that animals can learn language. First, animals must be able to use words. They must be able to use words without being told to do so. Washoe learned how to use over 250 different words. Washoe also learned how to <u>combine words</u> to make new thoughts. She came up with her own names for different things. She learned how to say these things <u>on her own</u>.

E

1. exhibit   2. monitor   3. symbol
4. feat   5. reinforce

Page 130

Step 1

Reading

Main idea: Animals can learn how to write language.
Key points:
- Studies have proven that animals can <u>learn language</u>.
- Also, animals can learn <u>how to write language</u>.

Lecture

Main idea: Kanzi the bonobo learned how to write.
Key points:
- He first had to learn <u>to understand language</u>.
  - Kanzi learned <u>symbols</u> called <u>lexigrams</u>.
  - In the woods, he touched <u>the lexigram for fire</u> and then made a fire.
- He then learned how to <u>write these symbols</u>.
  - At one point, Kanzi wanted to <u>go outside into the woods</u>.
  - He took a piece of chalk and <u>wrote the lexigram for woods</u>.

Page 131

Step 3

Topic: Whether animals can learn to write language.
A. The reading says that animals can learn how <u>to write language</u>.
  1. Studies have proven that <u>animals can learn language</u>.
  2. Also, animals can learn <u>how to write language</u>.
B. The lecture supports the reading by saying that Kanzi <u>learned how to write</u>.
  1. He first had to learn <u>to understand language</u>.
    • Kanzi learned <u>symbols called lexigrams</u>.
    • In the woods, he touched <u>the lexigram for fire and then made a fire</u>.
  2. He then learned how to <u>write these symbols</u>.
    • At one point, Kanzi wanted to <u>go outside into the woods</u>.
    • He took a piece of chalk and <u>wrote the lexigram for woods</u>.
Conclusion: Kanzi learned how to both <u>write symbols</u> and <u>know what they meant</u>.

Step 4

The reading and the lecture discuss <u>whether animals can learn language</u>. The reading says that animals <u>can learn how to write language</u>. Studies have proven that <u>animals can learn language</u>. Also, animals can learn <u>how to write language</u>.

The lecture supports the reading by saying that <u>Kanzi learned how to write</u>. First, he had to learn <u>to understand language</u>. Kanzi learned <u>symbols called lexigrams</u>. In the woods, he touched <u>the lexigram for fire and then made a fire</u>. Second, he learned how to <u>write these symbols</u>. At one point, Kanzi wanted to <u>go outside into the woods</u>. He took a piece of chalk and <u>wrote the lexigram for woods</u>.

Thus, the lecture supports the reading because it says that Kanzi learned how to both <u>write symbols</u> and <u>know what they mean</u>.

Check-up

Page 132

1. parrot   2. image   3. yield
4. ruin   5. stuck   6. combine
7. character   8. Sign language

[Review 2]

Independent 1

Page 133

Sample Answer 1
Step 2
agree

Answer Key

Step 3

Topic: Reading is <u>better for children</u> than playing video games.

A. <u>Reading is more educational than video games.</u>
   1. <u>There are many things you can read, like history books, famous literature, or poetry.</u>
   2. <u>I like reading more because I can learn about sea animals, which is what I want to study in the future.</u>
B. <u>Books are a lot more fun than video games.</u>
   1. <u>Books can tell really interesting and entertaining stories.</u>
   2. <u>I would rather enjoy a good story than a video game.</u>
Conclusion: This is why I think <u>children should read rather than play video games.</u>

Step 4

I think that reading <u>is better for children than playing video games.</u> To begin, I think <u>reading is more educational than video games.</u> I think that <u>there are many things you can read, like history books, famous literature, or poetry.</u> For example, <u>I like reading more because I can learn about sea animals, which is what I want to study in the future.</u> I also believe that <u>books are a lot more fun than video games.</u> I feel that <u>books can tell really interesting and entertaining stories. To me, I would rather enjoy a good story than a video game.</u>

This is why I think <u>children should read rather than play video games.</u>

Sample Answer 2
Step 2
<u>disagree</u>

Step 3

Topic: Reading is <u>not better for children</u> than playing video games.

A. <u>Video games can tell great stories too.</u>
   1. <u>Newer video games are more focused on telling a good story.</u>
   2. <u>One of my favorite games has a story as good as Star Wars.</u>
B. <u>Video games are more interactive than books are.</u>
   1. <u>Playing video games forces people to constantly make decisions and react to what is on the screen.</u>
   2. <u>Video games can teach children skills that books can't.</u>
Conclusion: This is why I think <u>video games aren't worse than books for children.</u>

Step 4

I think that reading <u>is not better for children than playing video games.</u> To begin, I think <u>video games can tell great stories too.</u> I think that <u>newer video games are more focused on telling a good story.</u> For example, <u>one of my favorite games has a story as good as Star Wars.</u> I also believe that <u>video games are more interactive than books are.</u> I feel that <u>playing video games forces people to constantly make decisions and react to what is on the screen. To me, video games can teach children skills that books can't.</u> This is why I think <u>video games aren't worse than books for children.</u>

Integrated 1

Page 134
Step 1

Reading

Main idea: Authors often create fiction stories by <u>writing about real people and events.</u>
Key points:
- Authors often use <u>real people that they know</u> to make fictional characters.
- To create a plot, authors sometimes use <u>real events from their lives.</u>

Lecture

Main idea: Mark Twain created The Adventures of Tom Sawyer by writing about <u>his childhood</u>.
Key points:
- Twain used <u>real people from his childhood</u> to make the characters in the book.
  - Tom Sawyer, the main character, is based on <u>Twain as a child</u>.
  - To make good characters, Twain decided to use <u>real people from his past.</u>
- Twain based the book's events on <u>real events from when he was a child</u>.
  - The book's story is about <u>Twain's life growing up</u>.
  - A scene where Tom's friends paint a fence was <u>based on a real event.</u>

Page 135
Step 3

Topic: The reading and the lecture discuss authors who use real events in fiction writing.

A. The reading discusses two ways that fiction writers <u>create stories using real people and events.</u>
   1. Authors often use <u>real people that they know</u> to make fictional characters.
   2. To create a plot, authors sometimes use <u>real events from their lives.</u>

B. The lecture <u>supports the reading</u> by discussing how Mark Twain wrote *The Adventures of Tom Sawyer*.
1. Twain used <u>real people from his childhood</u> to make the characters in the book.
   - Tom Sawyer, the main character, is based on <u>Twain as a child</u>.
   - To make good characters, Twain decided to use <u>real people from his past</u>.
2. Twain based the book's events on <u>real events from when he was a child</u>.
   - The book's story is about <u>Twain's life growing up</u>.
   - A scene where Tom's friends paint a fence was <u>based on a real event</u>.

Conclusion: The lecture <u>supports</u> the reading by <u>giving the example of Twain's famous novel</u>.

Step 4

The reading and the lecture both discuss <u>authors who use real events in fiction writing</u>. The reading discusses two ways that <u>fiction writers create stories using real people and events</u>. Firstly, authors often use <u>real people that they know to make fictional characters</u>. Secondly, to create a plot, authors sometimes use <u>real events from their lives</u>.

The lecture <u>supports the reading</u> by discussing <u>how Mark Twain wrote The Adventures of Tom Sawyer</u>. The speaker says that Twain used <u>real people from his childhood to make the characters in the book</u>. Tom Sawyer, the main character, is based on <u>Twain as a child</u>. To make good characters, Twain decided to use <u>real people from his past</u>. In addition, the speaker says that Twain based the book's events on <u>real events from when he was a child</u>. The book's story is about <u>Twain's life growing up</u>. A scene where Tom's friends paint a fence was <u>based on a real event</u>.

In conclusion, the lecture <u>supports the reading by giving the example of Twain's famous novel</u>.

Integrated 2

Page 136
Step 1
Reading

Main idea: The goal of the media is to <u>please the general public as much as possible</u>.
Key points:
- The entertainment media show <u>the programming that people want to see</u>.
- The media report the news that people <u>need the most</u>.

Lecture

Main idea: The aim of the media is <u>to make money</u>.
Key points:
- TV networks show things that <u>will make them the most money</u>.
  - The only reason for showing commercials is <u>to make money</u>.
  - Commercials do not serve <u>the public interest</u>.
- The point of <u>the news</u> is only to make money.
  - News stations and newspapers need to <u>make money</u>.
  - So they pick news that will <u>entertain</u> instead of <u>inform</u> people.

Page 137
Step 3

Topic: The reading and the lecture discuss whether the media serve the public interest.
A. The reading suggests that the media <u>try to please as much of the general public as possible</u>.
1. The entertainment media show <u>TV shows that people are most interested in</u>.
2. The media report the news that people <u>need to see the most</u>.
B. The lecture <u>disagrees with the reading</u> by offering two arguments.
1. TV networks show things that <u>will help them make money</u>.
   - The only reason for showing commercials is <u>to make money from them</u>.
   - Commercials do not serve <u>the public interest at all</u>.
2. The point of <u>the news</u> is only to make money.
   - News stations and newspapers need to <u>make money</u>.
   - So they pick news that will <u>entertain</u> instead of <u>inform</u> people.

Conclusion: The lecture <u>disagrees</u> with the reading by saying that <u>the point of the media is to make money, not serve the public interest</u>.

Step 4

The reading and the lecture discuss <u>whether the media serve the public interest</u>. The author of the passage says that the media <u>try to please as much of the general public as possible</u>. The author first says that entertainment media show <u>TV shows that people are most interested in</u>. Next, the author says that the media report <u>the news that people need to see the most</u>.

The lecture <u>disagrees with the reading</u> by offering <u>two points</u>. First, TV networks only show things that <u>will help them make money</u>. The only reason they show commercials is <u>to make money from them</u>.

Answer Key

Therefore, commercials do not <u>serve the public interest at all</u>. The speaker also says that the point of <u>the news is only to make money</u>. Newspapers and news stations <u>need to make money</u>. So they pick news that <u>will entertain instead of inform people</u>.

In conclusion, the lecture <u>disagrees with the reading by saying that the point of the media is to make money, not serve the public interest</u>.

Independent 2

Page 138

Sample Answer 1
Step 2
<u>agree</u>

Step 3
Topic: People who send many text messages, instant messages, and email <u>have</u> bad spelling.
A. <u>These things teach bad spelling habits.</u>
 1. <u>Texting encourages people to spell poorly so they can send messages faster.</u>
 2. <u>I don't always learn how to spell a word because I can just abbreviate it in an email.</u>
B. <u>People who text think that spelling isn't important.</u>
 1. <u>Most people who text don't care if their spelling is good or not.</u>
 2. <u>My friend sends me emails with bad spelling, but he doesn't care.</u>
Conclusion: This is why I think that <u>people who send a lot of typed messages have bad spelling.</u>

Step 4
I think that people <u>who send many text messages, instant messages, and email have bad spelling</u>. First, I think <u>these things teach bad spelling habits</u>. I believe that <u>texting encourages people to spell poorly so they can send messages faster</u>. When I send email, <u>I don't always learn how to spell a word because I can just abbreviate it in an email</u>. Secondly, I think <u>people who text think that spelling isn't important</u>. In my opinion, <u>most people who text don't care if their spelling is good or not</u>. For example, <u>my friend sends me emails with bad spelling, but he doesn't care</u>.

This is why I think that <u>people who send a lot of typed messages have bad spelling</u>.

Sample Answer 2
Step 2
<u>disagree</u>

Step 3
Topic: People who send many text messages, instant messages, and email <u>do not have</u> bad spelling.

A. <u>Texting and real writing are completely different things.</u>
 1. <u>People only spell words wrong in texts and emails because it is easier.</u>
 2. <u>I often use bad spelling, but I know how to spell those words the right way.</u>
B. <u>Many spelling errors in emails come from typos.</u>
 1. <u>Most people try to type really fast and might hit the wrong button.</u>
 2. <u>I often spell words wrong without realizing it, even though I know how they are spelled.</u>
Conclusion: This is why I think that <u>people who send a lot of typed messages don't always have bad spelling.</u>

Step 4
I think that people <u>who send many text messages, instant messages, and email do not have bad spelling</u>. First, I think <u>texting and real writing are completely different things</u>. I believe that <u>people only spell words wrong in texts and emails because it is easier</u>. When I send email, <u>I often use bad spelling, but I know how to spell those words the right way</u>. Secondly, I think <u>many spelling errors in emails come from typos</u>. In my opinion, <u>most people try to type really fast and might hit the wrong button</u>. For example, <u>I often spell words wrong without realizing it, even though I know how they are spelled</u>.

This is why I think that <u>people who send a lot of typed messages don't always have bad spelling</u>.

Worksheets Answer Key

[Unit 1] To-infinitives as Nouns

A
1. O
2. S
3. O
4. O
5. S
6. S
7. O
8. O

B
1. We also take them <u>to go</u> on picnics with us.
2. It is sad not <u>to care</u> about improving your relationship with your family.
3. His job is <u>to feed</u> the horses on the farm.
4. <u>To manage</u> its military properly was something that Rome failed at.
5. <u>To treat</u> pets as important as other family members is not good.
6. With a bad leader, fewer people wanted <u>to fight</u>.
7. They began <u>to reduce</u> the value of their money.
8. <u>To be</u> attacked many times can weaken a country's infrastructure.

C

(Answers will vary.)

1. I like to eat pizza when I am really hungry.
2. To go skating is my favorite thing to do on a cold winter day.
3. My chores at home are to wash the dishes and to clean my room.

[Unit 2] Gerunds

A

1. O   2. C   3. O   4. C
5. C   6. C   7. O   8. O

B

1. Building in different climates can change a design.
2. Some builders like using designs from history.
3. Asking to borrow money is awkward.
4. Stealing from friends is just not in her nature.
5. One thing to consider is transforming different materials to meet your purpose.
6. It is best to avoid disrupting the class during an exam.
7. You should consider repaying your loan early.
8. Could you gather the materials for making the bread?

C

(Answers will vary.)

1. I like drinking lemonade when I am really thirsty.
2. Swimming is my favorite thing to do on a hot summer day.
3. I have a friend who hates walking to school.

[Unit 3] Subject-Verb Agreement

A

1. was   2. are   3. is   4. helps
5. is   6. is   7. attracts   8. takes

B

1. Getting   2. To hold   3. To have
4. Pretending   5. To facilitate   6. borrowing

C

(Answers will vary.)

1. Playing chess requires a lot of concentration.
2. Rock-climbing and skiing are two difficult activities.
3. To play hockey in gym class and to read stories in English class are my two favorite school activities.
4. To lift weights needs a lot of strength.

[Unit 4] To-infinitives for Purpose

A

1. Some scientists use chemicals in order to preserve items they don't want to decay. ✓
2. The group used teamwork to accomplish their goals. ✓
3. The coach likes the team to practice for two hours each evening. __
4. Scientists can look at tree rings in order to calculate a tree's age. ✓
5. All living things begin to decay after they die. __
6. The whole team wants to have dinner at that restaurant. __
7. However, scientists can use other chemicals to remove the bad ones. ✓
8. Calibration uses other living things in order to find past rates of decay. ✓

B

1. to find   2. to make   3. to win   4. to fix
5. to meet   6. to treat   7. to enter   8. to learn

C

(Answers will vary.)

1. I study English in order to give myself a chance for a better job.
2. I brush my teeth to keep them clean.
3. I should exercise every day to stay healthy.

[Unit 5] Noun Clauses

A

1. Most people invest in businesses that they can trust. C
2. That he is the boss's nephew surely helped him get the job. S
3. That he rebels against his teachers now will not help him in the future. S
4. The girl that I met last night volunteers at the seniors' center. C
5. We need to come up with some healthy activities that teens can engage in. C
6. That you're learning to run a business now will be a great benefit in the future. S
7. That she is so young is not relevant to her ability to do the job. S
8. The movies that he adapted from her books generated millions of dollars. C

B

1. B   2. D   3. A   4. C

Answer Key

C
(Answers will vary.)
1. I hope that the weather will be nice this weekend.
2. That I can ride a unicycle makes me different than most people.
3. The food that your father cooked was really delicious.
4. There is a new movie coming out that the critics are highly recommending.

[Unit 6] Noun Clauses after Dummy Subjects

A
1. It is sad that many people in cities do not care about conservation. ✓
2. It is that idea that led to the theory of plate tectonics. ✓
3. It is over there, beside the park bench. __
4. That they teach people about nature is the reason we are here today. __
5. It should be a crime when animal populations are endangered. ✓
6. That people still continue to hunt them is at the heart of the issue. __
7. That we should be more aware of the damage we cause to nature is the point I am trying to make. __
8. Finally, it is important that people understand why it is necessary to conserve nature. ✓

B
1. It is better that animals be free to roam in nature.
2. It was really sad that the animals ran away.
3. It is important that we protect the animals regardless of the cost.
4. It is interesting that many people did not know it was possible for plates to move.

C
(Answers will vary.)
1. It is important that parents teach their children to be polite.
2. It is sad when people don't have enough money to buy food.
3. It is necessary that students study hard before a test.
4. It is frustrating when teachers assign too much homework.

[Unit 7] Noun Clauses with *Wh-* Words, *If*, and *Whether*

A
1. what   2. who   3. why   4. where
5. who   6. what   7. why   8. what

B
1. if we made reservations in the non-smoking section (or not).
2. whether (or not) I heard that myth before.
3. if cancer is the leading cause of death (or not).
4. whether (or not) he wants me to invite non-smoking guests.

C
1. I wonder whether (or not) people know the dangers of second-hand smoke (or not).
2. I don't know if the smoking ban is viewed by smokers to be a tragedy or not.
3. I can't decide whether (or not) I want to quit smoking (or not).
4. Whether (or not) the big tobacco companies had a motive (or not) is not important.

[Unit 8] Simple Past & Present Perfect

A
1. PP   2. SP   3. SP   4. PP
5. PP   6. SP   7. PP   8. PP

B
1. said   2. has designed
3. have had   4. have worked
5. went   6. has been
7. saved   8. spent

C
(Answers will vary.)
1. Yes. I used gas in my stove to boil water.
2. Yes. I have traveled to school by bike several times.
3. I have lived in this city for five years.
4. I started studying English three years ago.

[Unit 9] Basic Complex Sentences

A
1. When someone asserts something is correct on the Internet, it is up to the reader to second guess the assertion.
2. Journalism can be a rewarding career choice if it is taken seriously and respected.

3. If an Internet blog provides an account of something, it shouldn't necessarily be taken as fact.
4. I know what I read to be true because the information came from a news website.
5. This is a good thing because it makes it easier for people to talk with each other.

B
1. when
2. When
3. Because
4. before
5. Because

C
(Answers will vary.)
1. If I could change one thing about the Internet, I would make it faster to download large files.
2. I usually read comic books, whereas my parents usually read newspapers.
3. I enjoy playing tennis because it is fun and good exercise.
4. I sometimes get angry when my sister steals my money.

[Unit 10] Tense in Time and First Conditional Clauses

A
1. And when this happens, the law won't be true anymore.
2. After we create a camera and put it on the market, we begin creating one to replace it.
3. We should test the transistors before we ship them overseas.
4. When one computer gets faster, that means there are more to follow.
5. Our proportion of market share climbed after we introduced the improved model.
6. Before you go any further, you should research last year's trends.
7. You should buy a new computer after they introduce their new designs.
8. When this camera is launched, we will see gains in our stock price.

B
1. If we work hard on our company,
2. if we can't figure out how to fix these chips.
3. if I become rich.
4. If the company fails,

C
(Answers will vary.)
1. If the weather is rainy this weekend, I will go see a movie.

2. When I get hungry in the afternoon, I usually eat a piece of fruit.
3. If I study a lot for an exam, I get a high score on it.
4. When I don't get enough sleep, I get angry very quickly.

[Unit 11] Transitions for Logical Results

A
1. Therefore, he would naturally do good things. ✓
2. The Greeks tried to create a society that was ruled by the people; thus, democracy was born. ✓
3. They contain wisdom of former generations and give us a framework for how to live our lives. __
4. After, power was permanently in the hands of the people. __
5. For these reasons, democratic values were exported around the world. ✓
6. First, turn left at the next street; then walk straight for five minutes. ✓

B
1. Therefore, in order to live well we need only to review the law.
2. Thus, the people must know when and how to assert their power.
3. For these reasons, I think it is very valuable for people today to learn about the past.
4. Thus, you need to know about your history to understand your culture.

C
(Answers will vary.)
1. Once, I failed a math test because I didn't study for it
2. Another time, I studied hard and won an award for science
3. On my birthday, I got all the presents I wanted

[Unit 12] Transitions for Example, Emphasis, and Contrast

A
1. C
2. E
3. EX
4. C
5. C
6. E

B
1. On the other hand
2. However
3. conversely
4. In fact

C

1. The new buildings were battered by the storm; however, none of the old buildings were damaged.
2. They don't construct buildings well; indeed, the life expectancy of a new building is relatively short.
3. Most people enjoy modern style architecture; in contrast, I much prefer traditional buildings.
4. Many old apartment buildings were built before people had cars; on the other hand, new apartment buildings can be built with space for people to park their cars underground.